MID-CENTURY
MODERN

BRADLEY QUINN

MID-CENTURY MODERN

INTERIORS · FURNITURE · DESIGN DETAILS

For Bo and Maria

First published in 2004 by Conran Octopus Limited
a part of Octopus Publishing Group
2–4 Heron Quays, London E14 4JP
www.conran-octopus.co.uk

British Library Cataloguing-in-Publication Data. A catalogue
record for this book is available from the British Library.

ISBN 1 84091 406 8
Printed in China

Publishing Director: Lorraine Dickey
Art Director: Chi Lam
Executive Editor: Zia Mattocks
Art Editor: Megan Smith
Editor: Alison Wormleighton
Picture Research Manager: Liz Boyd
Picture Researcher: Clare Limpus
Special Photography: Graham Atkins Hughes & Stellan Herner
Styling for Special Photography: Bradley Quinn
Pattern Illustrator: Victoria Burley
Production Manager: Angela Couchman

contents

Introduction

Mid-century styles were left in the dark for nearly forty years as the spotlight shone on the electrifying styles of the rock 'n' roll generation and the cobwebs were blown off dusty retro designs from the 1960s and '70s. But with the dawn of the twenty-first century, mid-century pieces took centre stage once more as a design-conscious youth rediscovered their magic, and many 1950s classics seemed new again. A demand for objects whose sculptural and aesthetic qualities paralleled their functional attributes was on the rise, and many mid-century pieces became so popular that they seemed to overshadow contemporary designs.

The appeal of the mid-century period resurfaced during the 1990s, as a number of historic design currents made themselves felt. The painterly influence of the Bloomsbury Group in London, the minimalist, masculine look of Mies van der Rohe's tubular steel and leather furniture, the daring glamour of 1930s Paris captured in the designs of Jean Royère and Jean-Michel Frank, the pulsating graphics of Josef Hoffman's Vienna Secession and the stark silhouettes of Russian constructivism all spoke a timeless language that seemed strikingly contemporary. The spare aesthetics of Scandinavian designers, who introduced an indissoluble trinity of clean lines, functionalism and simplified forms, also enjoyed a renaissance. All these influences had actively shaped the distinctive style of the 1950s, as designers with backgrounds in architecture, fine art or graphic design pioneered the use of new materials, sculptural forms, novel colours and fluid motifs.

Although for many years the mid-twentieth century had been remembered as an era featuring endless variations of kitsch, during the 1990s the decade was also celebrated for its drive to simplify the interior, create more living space in the home and eliminate clutter, or at least hide it behind beautifully streamlined doors. The architectural minimalism of the 1950s was coupled with the organic modernism of the 1940s, resulting in an open-plan layout showcasing sleek structural elements crafted in natural materials. Houses shrank in size as parlours, formal dining rooms and grand entrance halls, now deemed superfluous, were absorbed by the open plan, ironically creating a greater sense of space as a result. Contemporary minimalism took the United States by storm as the Americans embraced the ideal of the unpretentious, modern interior that the new styles from Scandinavia seemed to represent.

RIGHT The open-plan living spaces of mid-century architecture eliminated walls and combined separate areas, radically transforming the way that domestic houses were structured. In this American home, built in Texas in 1956, an L-shaped space merges the living and dining areas with part of the kitchen. Although the George Nelson clock over the fireplace has ticked continuously for five decades, the interior has withstood the test of time.

Won over by its European cachet and celebration of natural materials. North Americans were introduced to Scandinavian design in 1954 via a touring exhibition entitled Design in Scandinavia. It proved to be a resounding success with the newly affluent middle classes, who were earnestly seeking an aesthetic orientation. The exhibition featured Danish furniture, along with glassware, ceramics, metalware and textiles from the other Nordic nations. To the bewilderment of the designers and their public back in Europe, the diverse output of the five Scandinavian countries was interpreted as a single style, and, despite the implicit paradox, the concept of a generic 'Scandinavian style' took hold.

Within the rationale of Scandinavian design was a mandate to beautify the interior through a choice of objects that would uplift its residents spiritually, making them feel better about their environment and their roles within it. These lofty principles were especially well suited to the American commitment to self-improvement and the drive to refine and improve the lives of others. Form and function were interpreted in stylistic terms but produced within a strict economic framework that made them affordable to those whose tastes were being reformed. Such a design ideology realized the goals advanced several decades earlier by Ellen Key in Sweden, and in Germany by the founders of the Bauhaus school of design, who fervently believed that good design could change the way people live and interact with each other.

In European eyes 1950s North America was also synonymous with privilege, excess and the glorious era of Hollywood glamour. American interiors flaunted popular culture and synthetic chic, juxtaposing elegant Knoll pieces with jukeboxes and neon signs, interspersing restrained Scandinavian classics among pieces with plastic veneers, fake fur and Formica surfaces. Framed photographs and unframed posters were pinned up on domestic walls, and many interiors also featured the commercial artworks that were mass-produced and sold in furniture stores.

As a creative centre, the United States yielded a prolific design milieu that advanced modern technology and pioneered the use of new materials, making it possible for designers to push out the boundaries of traditional craftsmanship. This resulted in a wide range of mass-produced multiples that contrasted sharply with refined, high-design pieces, both of which the Americans successfully mixed in interiors that fused the high with the low.

France, a country with a long history of being a leading arbiter of interior design, stood in vivid contrast to the restraint of Scandinavia and the minimalist architecture of North America. Most of the French population viewed the post-war interior with disdain, dismissing it as a sterile, mechanical and somewhat brutal style, and the government sponsored the Beauté de France award to perpetuate the lavish décor that had emerged during the 1920s and '30s. During the 1950s a preference for elaborate, overstated traditional bourgeois designs shaped French interiors, but a few designers, such as Charlotte Perriand, Jean Prouvé and René Herbst, pioneered modernist designs that became the icons of the era.

Although in 1951 Britain celebrated the talents of visionaries such as Robin and Lucienne Day and Ernest Race in the Festival of Britain, the country lagged behind. The British furniture industry continued to be regulated by the Utility Furniture Scheme, which enforced the strict standards introduced during the war years. Nevertheless, the Council of Industrial Design used the festival as an opportunity to promote the new 'contemporary style' among the general public.

While the Dutch followed North American designs more closely than those by their European counterparts, Italian designers created their own uniquely expressive style that transformed Italy into a visionary and influential destination. Venetian glass was radically updated with sinuous shapes and incandescent colours, and Italian furniture and industrial designs communicated in the same dynamic visual language.

Today mid-century classics from all parts of the world are enjoying a revival, and they symbolize an emerging trend to renew the language and culture of modernism. A large number of classic designs have remained in continuous production since they were originally launched, and many provide a source of inspiration for today's designers. The timeless appeal of the era shows that mid-century design was not just a fleeting historical phenomenon, but an aesthetic that will have allure well into the future. Many classic designs have been elevated to the status of cultural artefacts in today's interiors. As they are remembered for revolutionizing the way people lived, they represent a return to an optimistic vision of modern life.

In homes ranging from urban apartments to rural retreats, *Mid-Century Modern* goes behind the closed doors of private collectors to reveal how today's interiors can engage with another era and yet appear utterly contemporary. From chapters dedicated to furniture design to specialist sections on ceramics, glassware, metalware and tableware, the history of 1950s design unfolds through descriptions of the period's leading pieces and the significance of their continued appeal. The book features landmark architecture, inventive space planning and the beauty of natural materials, as well as many compelling pictures of homes in which mid-century style has been successfully adapted to today's lifestyles. As an inspirational guide to living with iconic designs and introducing a modernist mood to the home, the book provides a fascinating lexicon of one of the twentieth century's most enduring styles.

THE MID-CENTURY HOME

Long before today's trend for minimal living took hold, the cool, laconic interiors of the mid-twentieth century were characterized by their understated beauty and fluid interpretation of space.

The contemporary 1950s interior was never intended to be static, but was conceived as a dialogue between the flooring, furniture and lighting and the dynamics of the architecture itself. The mid-century home was designed to facilitate modern life, with an interior flexible enough to accommodate modern lifestyles.

The decorating ideals of the post-war era were inspired by modernist principles, which were translated by architects and designers into a timeless aesthetic based on balance, natural elements and stylistic harmony. The interiors of the 1950s made full use of the forms and principles introduced by the modernists three decades earlier, ushering in a fresh vision of domestic life based on an economy of space as well as materials. Functional furniture, space planning and expressive designs provided the perfect glue to hold the mid-century interior together.

In previous decades contemporary décor had been essentially shaped by urban experience, where new visions for modern living unfolded. Visionaries such as Mies van der Rohe, Charles Eames, Arne Jacobsen and Eero Saarinen conceived of a uniform domestic architecture that would easily integrate into the cityscape and yet sit comfortably against a rural backdrop. The focus of modern architecture lost its European bias, becoming an international movement whose flagships were built in the United States in the post-war years. While Europeans were rebuilding lost landmarks, Americans were taking domestic architecture swiftly forward.

As architects embraced new concepts of modern dwellings, many of their ideas unfolded through the use of natural materials such as wood, stone and brick. The new housing styles displayed a preference for clean, uncluttered lines coloured in muddy earth tones or dusty pastels. Bricks were contrasted with plaster, while glass, wood cladding and sheets of metal took on a new decorative role as their shiny surfaces and rough textures were deployed to break down the scale of the facade. Some of the architectural details that debuted in the iconic villas of the 1920s and '30s were introduced to mainstream homes, making exposed structural supports, glass exterior walls, built-in furniture and open-plan living areas standard features.

The home became a welcoming haven of easy comforts, and by the end of the decade most households were fully mechanized and ultra-efficient, setting new standards for maintenance and renewal. The American home was the most progressive in this respect, and the American kitchen was bursting with technical innovations and new appliances that made it the envy of every housewife around the world. Informal styles of eating and dining emerged in the 1950s, largely because architects and interior designers took a fresh look at the possibilities offered by living space and reassessed the needs of the modern family. Furniture and household accessories were as comfortable as they were affordable, and designed to reflect the new architecture. Items that sported a luxurious look but were also functional obliterated the distinction between everyday objects and those reserved for special occasions. Likewise, the notion of reserving rooms for special occasions was replaced by the idea of living in a house where all spaces were for daily use.

The drive to update and improve the home took hold at this time, ultimately resulting in the trend of fast-changing decorating fads that we regard as the norm today. Publications such as *Interiors*, *Domus*, *Tomorrow's House*, *House Beautiful* and *House & Garden* had a high circulation in the 1950s, and these magazines presented modernist interiors as paragons of domestic bliss. Feature articles showed readers how innovative design techniques and new materials such as fibreglass, plastic laminates and latex foam could redefine the home.

Nowhere in the glossy images of these interior landscapes did a shadow of melancholy fall to dispel the vision of familial accord; the modern family found validation and expression in the objects with which they surrounded themselves. The open floor plan united all members of the family in the same room, yet created spaces for individuals in the zones for different activities designated within it. The living space, along with its furniture, was flexible, adaptable, well organized and at all times superbly maintained – apt metaphors for the housewife's role and the code of conduct observed by those who lived there. As mid-century homemakers readily embraced the latest styles of design, they acquired a visual and tactile awareness that resonated beyond the interior to create an aesthetic framework around daily life.

This new concept of 'home' is in many respects the key to the mid-century interior. Its careful craftsmanship, perfection, harmony and natural feeling were seen as the dream of a better world – in a Europe that had risen from the devastation of the Second World War, and in a North America still recovering from the Depression and shaking off the frugalities of the war years.

As the decade passed, the 1950s interior left behind a legacy of textures, motifs, streamlined forms and unadulterated shapes that remain as practical as they are beautiful. This uncompromising vision of domestic life has persisted for more than half a century, evolving into the iconic mid-century style we regard as timeless today.

The American dream

Bigger homes, sleeker décor, more space, less clutter – the interiors of the 1950s presented a fresh vision of what houses could be, and changed for ever the idea of what the home should look like. The rich textures, colourful tints and polished wood grains of the mid-century home created a sense of exuberance and vitality that continued to have an impact for many decades to follow. Modern equipment gave the home a high-tech feel and made domestic tasks less onerous, enabling the occupants to enjoy more leisure time in their spacious, open-plan interiors. A happy family and a big car completed the comfortable, carefree lifestyle that became known as 'the American dream', and the home was its very embodiment.

Mid-century homes were inhabited by a new generation of Americans, who altered their expectations of the home as they grew to appreciate novel types of living spaces and the landscapes surrounding them. Young American home-owners eschewed conventional ideas of what houses should look like and how they should be lived in, turning away from traditional styles and family heirlooms. The North American home had never before been so completely modern – antiques and period styles virtually disappeared from the interior for an entire decade as householders concentrated on achieving a completely contemporary 'look' for their homes.

The contemporary American home of the 1950s was designed to function as both an intimate family environment and an elegant setting for the owners' collection of furniture and decorative objects. Homemakers purchased functional items that were crafted in beautiful forms. They shopped for streamlined furniture that was produced with linear simplicity, contoured into sculptural shapes or designed as biomorphic forms (boomerang shapes, parabolas, ellipses, rhomboids – see page 92), and as they did so, they developed a deeper understanding and appreciation of design.

Although the home was a showcase for beautiful new objects, it was also a laboratory of technological progress. Modern machinery adjusted the temperature and regulated water pressure, while sleek vacuum cleaners, panel-controlled lighting systems, transistor radios and stereo hi-fis made technical innovations a part of domestic life. Food was prepared with the assistance of modern appliances, and homes were equipped with electric cookers, double ovens, washing machines and refrigerators that could produce ice and tenderize meat.

LEFT Built with a view over the Hollywood Hills, this mid-century bungalow was designed with panoramic windows that bring the surrounding vistas into the home. The architects placed the kitchen in the core of the home, with the dining area and living room spiralling around it to connect to the landscape on broad terraces.

ABOVE RIGHT Mid-century American kitchens were equipped with new appliances that simplified domestic tasks and raised the expectations of house-wives around the world.

The American public wanted modest family houses based on simple, accessible layouts, such as those developed by functionalist architects in Scandinavia and continental Europe. Although American architects were rediscovering the merits of Shaker simplicity, the streamlined interior style was largely attributed to Scandinavian functionalism. While the construction boom of the post-war era enabled the country to develop at an unprecedented rate, the United States was still a nation lacking an aesthetic orientation. European architects such as Mies van der Rohe, Eliel Saarinen, Walter Gropius and Marcel Breuer played a key role in reinterpreting the high-minded architectural principles of Europe in a style that would appeal to American tastes.

American architects began developing flexible designs that could be easily adapted for a range of landscapes. They conceived of low, rambling bungalows that hugged the landscape and split-level homes that could embrace a gentle slope or could be cantilevered dramatically from a hillside. The flat-roof bungalows of the Southwest and West Coast contrasted sharply with the pitched-roof houses of the East Coast and the Midwest. The mild winters of California and the Southwest meant that an 'indoor/outdoor' lifestyle was possible all year round, in homes built around courtyards or designed with several patios that integrated the house with the landscape.

Choice of house style was not determined just by the landscape or the climate. Many North American housing developers catered to conservative home-owners who believed that the modern style was a trend that would quickly fade, with the houses

BELOW LEFT This house in Beverly Hills was designed to shield the south-facing interior from the harsh rays of the sun, yet make the north view over the San Fernando Valley the focal point of the home. Concrete slabs extend the dining area onto the patio outside.
ABOVE RIGHT The relationship between the house and the garden was central to 1950s architecture. Glass walls and doorways made patios integral to the home.
ABOVE FAR RIGHT This breakfast bar continues its circle beyond the boundary walls to increase the living area. Cypress boards panel the exterior, and the interior reaches all the way to the roof.

dropping in value as a result. Traditional styles, such as the shuttered, pitch-roofed 'Cape Cod' house that was popular throughout the 1920s and '30s, were updated and reintroduced. Some developers built pitch-roofed, 'traditional' styles on wide, curving streets, while prohibiting the use of garden walls and fences in order to foster a sense of community among new neighbours.

Houses like these, along with many flat-roofed mid-century houses, were designed to be built as quickly and as economically as possible. Architects experimented with prefabricated panels and metal frames, refining and accelerating mass-production techniques to enable thousands of identical homes to be built in a single year. Suburban communities were constructed on tracts of land crisscrossed by street after street of identical houses. As rural areas were converted to tract housing, vast expanses of suburbia spread across the United States. New parts of a city could include several large-scale housing developments, known as sub-divisions. In some instances, such as Panorama City in Los Angeles and Park Forest outside Chicago, the entire development was built by a single construction company.

Among the most enduring mid-century designs were the 'ranch-style' houses that flourished on the West Coast. As early as 1945, nine noted architects in Los Angeles embarked on a quest to design prototypes of modern, progressive houses, the most famous being Richard Neutra and Charles Eames. These 'Case Study' homes, as they became known, had a huge impact on 1950s residential designs. The Case Study houses were scientific triumphs: they had been designed in a laboratory and tested on inhabitants of all ages before being built for the masses. Pared down to their essence, they were designed to melt into the landscapes where they were built. Architectural components were crafted in materials such as redwood, teak and oak, and highlighted in both the facades and the interiors. The houses' streamlined, reductivist designs appealed to professional families of average incomes, providing style-conscious alternatives to steel-framed houses with standardized prefabricated parts.

The Case Study architects eliminated interior walls and even cut away ceilings, establishing transparency as a standard theme in the contemporary interior. Open-plan designs afforded views over several rooms in a single visual sweep, while split-level plans enabled separate floors to interconnect more easily. Wide landings were positioned to afford views over the living areas, linked by open-tread staircases that transmitted light between floors. Sash or casement windows disappeared as single

[The mid-century home was designed as an ongoing visual dialogue involving all aspects of the interior – architecture, lighting, furniture, flooring – to create a sense of balance and harmony throughout.]

sheets of glass were fitted in their place, and pairs of windows were replaced by large glass panels that eliminated the need for networks of windowpanes. Generous windows overlooked the flowerbeds and gardens outside, flooding the interior with light diffused through sheers stretching from floor to ceiling. Panels of thick glass were sometimes built in order to divide interiors vertically without interrupting the view.

A dense brick support wall often separated the kitchen from the living and dining areas, typically giving an open, wood-burning fireplace with a high hearth pride of place in the centre. Rectangular in shape and fitted without a mantelpiece or even exterior ornamentation, it was positioned so as to be the pivot of the home, a concept that Frank Lloyd Wright had introduced decades earlier.

Cross walls (supporting walls running from front to back) were built in brick or stone to enclose parts of the interior, integrating the house's structural supports with the interior architecture. The structural details visible in the interior were presented in an understated manner that emphasized the materials more than the construction techniques. Elegant curves appeared to overtake right angles at every turn, and even kitchen worktops and architectural trim were gently contoured rather than rectilinear.

Panels of wooden trellis were sometimes used as partitions to create separate areas within an open-plan space, and open shelving units were often employed in a similar way. By incorporating display areas within the interior architecture, less free-standing furniture was needed, allowing the home-owners to make more efficient use of the living space. Storage compartments, concealed behind sliding doors with louvred slats or panelled surfaces, eliminated the need for wardrobes, bureaus and other visible storage pieces. Multi-purpose units provided additional storage for everyday items, and were often crafted in materials such as teak or designed as part of the interior woodwork. Built-in cupboards with drop-leaf doors were made to provide drinks cabinets with bar surfaces, or to double as work surfaces and writing desks.

The open-plan living and dining areas usually had ceilings as high as the eaves and were situated several steps lower than the rest of the home to create even greater volume. They were typically sited at the back of the house for immediate access to the garden, patio and brick barbecue. The flagstone flooring, ceramic tiles or polished brick of the living areas typically continued onto the patio outside, generating a continuous dialogue between the interior and the landscape outside.

Scandinavian modernism

Although the modernist philosophy of clarity, simplicity and functionality revolutionized the design traditions of mid-century continental Europe and North America, its basic precepts had, in fact, been defining features of the Scandinavian home for several decades. Modernism was not merely a decorative and architectural style; it had become a system of living involving tightly woven spatial connections between architecture, interior design, furniture and household accessories.

The decade of the 1950s was a dynamic time for domestic architecture. Although Scandinavian architects modified the functionalistic style that had dominated the pre-war period, the emphasis on the efficient use of space remained. In addition, mid-century interiors were characterized by a prevalence of natural materials and by the subtle treatment of light, in urban apartments, grand villas and modest houses alike. Modernism was a mantra for Scandinavian living, but there continued to be a reverence for traditional materials.

All Scandinavian countries underwent substantial social and economic changes during the post-war era, evolving into strong welfare states with generous subsidies available for housing. Sweden was the first to achieve an economic recovery, largely because of its neutrality during the war, and throughout the 1950s it constituted a mecca for modern design. Neither opulent architecture nor luxurious homes were important; outstanding craftsmanship, beautiful materials and design excellence were. Houses and apartment buildings were practical and functional, designed to maximize the use of space through open-plan living areas and well-planned storage.

For several decades before the war, Norway and Finland had been building streamlined functionalistic houses alongside elaborate National Romantic-style villas – noted for their turrets, towers, balconies, decorative detailing and vernacular elements – but by the 1950s a progressive, modernist style dominated. Both nations advocated efficiency in the home, with Finland the first to promote the mid-century home as a completely new model

RIGHT Since the early twentieth century, Nordic countries had been building streamlined functionalistic houses, and by the 1950s architects such as Alvar Aalto were promoting a new model of living, based on the open plan. As this Paris interior shows, even some French mid-century homes were built and furnished in the influential style.

for living, one that bridged the gulf between everyday needs and ideals of comfort, efficiency, style and beauty. Norwegian architects were also aesthetically inclined, but they were rather more rational than the Finns, insisting that form should follow function. Norwegian homes balanced luxury and relaxation with the practicality of streamlined styles that were economical to produce and easy to maintain.

The architect and designer Arne Jacobsen returned to Denmark after the war and immediately laid plans for a new type of interior, which he perfected first in his own home, completed in 1950. Here, he eliminated superfluous interior walls and built double-height ceilings, creating open-plan vistas interrupted only by furniture of his own design. Long pendant lamps and sculptural mobiles hung above tile flooring that covered the ground floor in a bold ceramic grid. Jacobsen divided some parts of the interior with windowless cross walls built in brick. The living-room walls, which faced the seafront, were punctured with glass panels that framed the panorama over the Baltic.

Many Danes abandoned the restrained simplicity of early modernism and built homes similar to Jacobsen's, incorporating robust colours, sensuous materials and a wide range of decorative details. The new housing styles were angular in profile and slightly industrial in plan. Bricks were contrasted with plaster or roughcast surfaces, while materials such as corrugated panels, wood cladding and sheets of metal took on a new decorative role, as colours and textures were deployed to break up the facade, thereby reducing its scale.

Scandinavian architects of the 1950s advocated individuality, intimacy and smallness of scale, enabling clients to shape the orientation of their houses and make their own aesthetic choices. Apartment buildings were built with flexible floor plans that would give residents a range of different options as their families grew over time. Many apartments included movable partition walls, while some buildings were planned according to an elastic principle that would allow a small studio apartment on each floor to be added to one of the others if expansion was needed.

In Sweden a standard-sized apartment of 56 square metres (600 square feet) could accommodate three rooms, designed to be used in line with the principle of flexible space. A galley kitchen opened into the living area, alongside a dining area constructed so that it could easily be converted into another bedroom if necessary, with the dining table moved into the living room. Often the dining area was enclosed by glass to create

LEFT The style we regard as Scandinavian today can be traced back to the mid-century era, when architects and designers conceived the home as a sleek environment for leisure and comfort. Here, Finn Juhl's classic NV-45 armchair and two-seater sofa fit in well with the minimalist interior.
ABOVE RIGHT Mid-century architects created sweeping walls of windows to channel all available light into the home, an important consideration during the long, dark Scandinavian winters.

[Scandinavian mid-century décor, with its clean lines, natural materials and light, bright spaces, continues to look contemporary in the twenty-first century. Scandinavian style is enduring and timeless in its appeal.]

a private space for overnight guests or a semi-private workroom. By the end of the decade, however, the belief that the home could grow with the family proved unrealistic, because each resident used his or her full allocation of space from the start.

High-rise urban apartment buildings were often built in so-called star-shaped configurations, which actually looked more like three interlocking tripod shapes. The star plan maximized the surface area of the outer walls, eliminating the need for an inner courtyard to provide light. In a region where winters are long and dark, it was necessary to harness every ray of sunlight and draw it indoors. The star plan provided two-storey apartments, usually allocating only three apartments per two floors. The plan ingeniously channelled daylight into the apartment from four points of the compass just as a detached house would. Windows were crafted from wide panes of double-glazed glass set within simple brickwork facades or modest roughcast exteriors.

Contained within Sweden's unpretentious exteriors was an ideologically explosive force. Planners and architects argued that living space should be measured not by the number of rooms but by the floor area. They demanded that the Swedish welfare state make municipal amenities available to all urban residents. The result was mid-century apartment buildings with communal facilities, such as workshops, playgrounds, storage areas and laundry rooms. Large complexes often also included lending libraries and childcare facilities, and specially commissioned mosaics and wall murals.

Single-family houses of the 1950s were for the most part simple two-storey boxes, built in the Brutalist style popular during the early years of the decade. The exterior walls consisted of single brick walls, daringly thin, interrupted by bands of windows with visible lintels over them, topped by gently sloping roofs constructed without projecting eaves or dormer windows. Bedrooms were placed on the upper floor and illuminated by high windows set in the gable walls. Balconies and porticos were built outwards from the facade as if they were free-standing structures. Likewise, the garage was housed in a separate building rather than integrated with the house.

The front doorway opened into a small entry hall, where an open-tread wooden staircase rose upwards along the expanse of a structural wall. In the interior, wood trim was used to lift the architectural features of the rooms, while tracts of polished stone seemed to anchor the house to the bedrock beneath it. Vertical panelling, crafted from pine, fir, larchwood, birch, oak and spruce, enhanced the interior with subtle textures

ABOVE RIGHT The unassuming interiors of Scandinavian homes spawned an influential international style. Interior walls were eliminated and small windows replaced by large glass panels. Instead of bulky curtains, roller blinds (shades) covered the windows in fabric panels that disappeared overhead when rolled up. The walls were panelled and the ceiling was covered in a weightless canopy of blond wood.

and a natural sheen. The panelling clad the interior in broad planks or lined the ceiling in a sleek canopy of wood grain. The lightness of the pale woods contrasted with the density of the stone floor and fireplace, filling the interior with the distinctive visual textures of materials harvested from the landscapes of the far north.

Inexpensive single-storey houses were constructed according to a design that could grow with a family from a basic blueprint of 84 square metres (900 square feet). The core of the home was open plan, with a partition wall separating the kitchen from the living area. Small, galley-like bedrooms were accessed from a single corridor opening off the main room. These rooms featured compact walk-in wardrobes that provided storage for clothing, suitcases and sports equipment. By removing the need for heavy chests and wardrobes, walk-in wardrobes provided unobtrusive storage that hid clutter from view.

The style of living enjoyed by the people of Scandinavia today can be traced back to the mid-century era, when architects and designers created an uncompromising new vision of what domestic life could be. The home was conceived as a place where leisure interests and social activities could unfold within a family milieu, or in dwellings for single people and couples. While the living environment was seen as a means of shaping everyday life, it was also designed to be comfortable and liberating.

European style

The principles of modernism that had taken hold among architects and designers in North America had their origins in pre-war Europe, but mid-century European designers were struggling to reclaim them. In the aftermath of the war, materials were scarce and skilled workshops few and far between. The housing boom that swept North America did not arrive in Europe until the mid-1950s, making the market for new products cripplingly limited. Government incentives were launched to revive the construction industry and spark a demand for household goods, but for many, new homes and contemporary décor remained out of reach.

Against this background, designers and architects still managed to create new housing schemes and furnish them with a fresh look. Many designers relied on labour-intensive hand production until industrial manufacturing was revived, leading to specialist products with individuality. Lack of materials fostered a climate of innovation and experimentation that might not have occurred otherwise. Necessity eclipsed luxury, and the demand for beautiful everyday objects ushered in the streamlined, functional style popular in the Nordic countries.

However, while Scandinavian style influenced the interiors of southern Europe, it never had the same impact that it had on the North American home. In Europe elements of Scandinavian design were juxtaposed with the ultra-luxurious styles influenced by American 'retro' exports, and the expressive, energetic, colourful interiors of the Mediterranean.

With their long-established history as leaders in ornamental design and decorative arts, the French never felt comfortable with the pared-down modernism introduced in the 1950s. In France the concept of functionalism was largely ignored by young homemakers, and the minimalist principle of bare surfaces was regarded as austere and impoverished. France had a unique sense of design, and modernism, like art deco, was seen as a luxury style tempered with historical influences and limited to a moneyed minority. The French had mastered revival styles centuries earlier, and homemakers turned to new interpretations

LEFT Considered to be a modernist masterpiece, Le Corbusier's Villa Sarabhai was built in India in 1956 with a robust structure of concrete and stone. Wood panelling, blond woodwork and rich colours soften the dense interior architecture, while pivoting doors and retractable lamps diffuse the light in the interior.

of traditional styles to decorate the mid-century interior in an expressive manner. Marble and polished stone lined the floor with a lustrous sheen, while wrought iron was used to fashion elaborate interior screens and room dividers, ornate door grilles and sweeping light fittings. Sumptuous textiles such as velvet and damask featured alongside thick plywood and straw marquetry, imparting an ambience of low-key luxury.

In Britain, many homemakers turned to exhibitions such as the Festival of Britain in 1951 and the annual Ideal Home Show in London, which educated the public in how to furnish basic apartments economically. Presenting contemporary architecture, interiors, household accessories and graphic motifs, these events were intended to inspire young home-owners and give the British public renewed confidence in its interior design.

For many Britons the economical social housing that was built by local governments in regenerated areas and in new towns provided the only modern housing within their reach. These council estates, whether they were comprised of houses or of small apartments, were for the most part featureless and austere. They were synonymous with the post-war Labour government's visions of socialist modernism, and were far removed from the relative comfort and luxury afforded by new housing schemes in the rest of Europe. Out of necessity, home-owners adopted streamlined, functional furniture to maximize the available space, and decorated the interiors with colourful textiles that masked the concrete structure and screened out the ubiquitous brown-brick exteriors.

A typical two-bedroom modern apartment would have been built across two levels, mirroring the traditional 'two up, two down' terraced house inhabited by working families across the country. The front door opened into a small entrance hall that gave way to a tiny, efficient kitchen situated on one side and an open-plan living area beyond. The kitchen 'hatch' opened into the large room, enabling the two rooms to communicate and making it easier to pass food into the eating area. An open-tread staircase, built in wood or in concrete, led to the floor above, accessing the bedrooms and a small bathroom. The second bedroom usually opened onto a small balcony to give a feeling of greater space, with built-in cupboards placed in the wall shared by the master bedroom. Downstairs, the living area opened onto a larger balcony, or a terrace if the apartment was on the ground floor, with storage space limited to the kitchen cabinets or the hall cupboard.

ABOVE Contemporary Mediterranean homes were filled with energetic colours and lively motifs, and often featured American 'luxury' exports.
RIGHT Principles of efficiency governed the mid-century kitchen, where a breakfast bar saved space. Like a hatch, it also provided an opening through which food could be passed and allowed the kitchen and living areas to communicate while clearly demarcating the areas.

[A new concept of restrained opulence unfolded during the 1950s, when streamlined, simplified interiors were regarded as the height of luxury.]

Affluent houses were often built with facades of red brick, trimmed with panels of oiled cedar. Smooth glass panels replaced exterior walls in some places, providing the perfect foil for heavy stone cross walls constructed in granite or flagstone. Iron balustrades with polished mahogany capping flanked the entrance, and continued to curve upwards to the floors above, or quickened into a looping spiral staircase. Exterior windows were conceived as glazed screens, often combining both clear and translucent glass in a casement frame of painted softwood.

Indoors, unpainted wooden units, such as shelving and built-in cupboards, were crafted in polished hardwood above smooth floorboards, rubber tiles or shiny linoleum. The overall impression was one of understatement and restraint, which became a hallmark of the British mid-century interior.

Italian homes, on the other hand, possessed novelty, vitality and artistic élan. The contemporary Italian interior, characterized by its strong silhouettes, vibrant colours and curvaceous forms, became an essential part of urban culture. Italy was unique in that progressive design had great impact outside the home, surrounding the Italians throughout their daily lives. Modernism sparked a design revolution that started in the home and resonated outwards, shaping the aesthetics of Italy's regeneration. The contours of furniture, lighting, household accessories and domestic utensils were mirrored in designs like the Pavoni espresso machine and the Visetta sewing machine. Even business centres and public offices sported equipment that looked domestic; designers such as Ettore Sottsass moved between interior styling and industrial design.

Architects like Carlo Mollino, Gio Ponti, Carlo de Carli and Gianfranco Frattini designed both buildings and furniture, creating interiors that linked the house's structure to the designs of its furniture. Quarried marble was laid underfoot in terrazzo patterns polished to a high gloss, or gave way to bold Pirelli flooring. Interiors were suffused with primary hues. Surrealistic furniture designs transformed everyday objects into pieces of sculpture and were surrounded by expressionistic textile motifs that resembled geometric forms or organic abstractions.

Interior details like floors, windowsills, cabinets, and balustrades were crafted in traditional materials such as wood, metal, stone and woven cane, which featured alongside coloured plastics, patterned Formica, tubular steel and moulded plywood. The Italians had been the first in Europe to experiment with new materials. Many parts of Italy were devastated by the war, and innovation was essential to compensate for the scarcity of materials. For much of the 1950s, Italy's design output remained true to its tradition of small-scale, hand-produced craftsmanship, which produced a wider range of style variations than in countries that had adapted more quickly to mass production.

Italian homes featured open-plan areas, which generally remained partially divided into separate zones by half-walls, partitions, archways or other architectural devices. Bulky compartmentalized furniture continued to be made and remained on view rather than being replaced by built-in storage. Cabinets and sideboards were crafted in metal or wood, while free-standing shelving and glass vitrines provided elegant display areas. Staircases were designed for theatrical impact, with sweeping balustrades and curvaceous outlines. As Italian designers took inspiration from the lavishness of the 1930s to create the streamlined chic of the 1950s, they produced interiors dazzling enough to eclipse the turbulent memories of the intervening decade.

The irrefutable Italian quality of urban décor mirrored the demand for popular symbols of Italy's contemporary culture. National feeling in the 1950s was strong and flourished throughout all the arts, finding expression in the textiles, furniture and interior features of the houses designed or decorated during the period. The industrial progress that characterized the decade was considered by many Italians to be a great leap forward, and the new interior style literally brought such sentiments closer to home.

Today the Italians look back on the 1950s as a period of unsurpassed design innovation, a time when the nation was engaged in the pursuit of *la dolce vita*. Their quest for the accoutrements of the good life presented an exciting rationale for living that Italian interiors continue to exemplify in the twenty-first century.

INTERIOR DECOR

The mid-century interior introduced a flexible and efficient aesthetic that modernized every aspect of the home and made colours and motifs central to the indoor landscape.

In the 1950s the roles of construction materials, textiles and lighting within the home were reassessed, creating a new interior defined by the needs of a changing lifestyle. Whereas these design genres had previously been regarded as separate entities, they came together for the first time as parts of a harmonious whole. Sharing ideas and often producing designs for more than one genre, mid-century designers worked together to create new, and sometimes startling, interpretations of how the modern home should be furnished and decorated.

The interrelatedness of all household items was fundamental to the mid-century interior. The open-plan layout dictated that the space be divided without the use of walls, and the alignment of furniture was an unobtrusive means of dividing the home into separate living areas. The careful positioning of carpets and sculptural objects reinforced this 'zoning'. It was necessary for lighting to relate to furniture, and so it became as flexible as any other element, if not more so. Colour and motifs were now perceived as outstanding features rather than background elements.

Architects worked with incredible sensitivity to integrate homemakers fully with the structure of their homes. The proportions of the house were regarded as mysterious determinants of the degree of intimacy; although the positioning of doorways, corridors and staircases was determined architecturally, generous space was allocated for the placement of furniture so that the interior never felt cramped or congested. Indeed, space was husbanded like a precious resource, with every cupboard and compartment organized and accounted for. Discreet storage solutions were provided throughout the home, offering ways to keep surfaces streamlined and clutter-free. Space planning became absolutely key.

Mid-century houses, whether built in contemporary or in traditional styles, were smaller than their predecessors, and as a result they needed slimmer, more efficient furniture. Contemporary pieces mirrored the new architectural style and were constructed in many of the same materials. Furniture designs and textile motifs generally remained true to the parallel lines and grid patterns of the architecture, and many of their shapes were geometric and linear. Although the seamless coordination between them created a sleek aesthetic, the interior required careful layering of colours, textures, patterns and soft furnishings to prevent a sterile look.

Interior designers counteracted the excessive rectilinear shapes with sinuous, organic textures that offset the abundance of right angles, and used contrasting colours, large-scale motifs and bold wallpaper repeats to impart a greater sense of depth. In contrast to the gravitas and stillness of minimalism, vibrant cushion covers, upholstery, wall hangings, table runners and fabric throws injected colour and movement into every part of the home. Soft furnishings featured abstract floral patterns; designs inspired by crystalline structures seen under a microscope; sci-fi motifs of comets, stars or solar systems; geometric prints of wide circles, segments or parallel lines; or polka dots in sugary pinks, reds, blues and yellows. Animal prints, especially zebra stripes and leopard spots, abounded on furnishing fabrics or as fake-fur cushions. Solid-colour fabrics were used for upholstery, cushions or curtains to give contrasting or coordinating planes of colour within the open plan.

The look for the contemporary home had a strong urban signature. It was an environment that embraced innovation at every level, even down to the owner's taste in art forms. The 1950s ushered in a new era of art, and the homemaker was expected to include works that referenced the abstract expressionism that was sweeping the United States. Paintings and sculptures brought the art movement closer to home, while expressionistic prints and lithographs were also framed and put on display. Paintings of the period were characterized by splashes of bright pigments and streaks of iridescent colour executed on wide canvases or stretched onto oversized square frames. Sculptures in stone, bronze or wood revealed the popularity of organic forms on the theme of gestation, such as the nut in the shell and the child in the womb.

Urban chic filtered through to rural American towns and suburbs via the pages of glossy magazines, or was introduced to prospective home-owners when they visited model homes on suburban housing developments. Impeccably furnished, these showcased the designs that were revolutionizing the 1950s and revealed how new products should be used. Model homes showed how furniture should be arranged and where lighting should be placed. Also revealing that the contemporary home was an environment for entertaining guests, they created a pleasantly louche atmosphere for playing cards, serving canapés, mixing cocktails and smoking cigarettes.

In Europe initiatives such as the Festival of Britain in 1951 and H55 in Helsingborg, Sweden in 1955 acted as platforms for young architects and designers to display their talents. These events boosted local confidence by showing that design and industry were moving forward. Such festivals made the new style more acceptable to the general public, demonstrating the importance of colour, materials, textiles and lighting in the landscape of the modern domestic interior.

Minimalism & maximalism

'Start from scratch' was the dictum issued by many architects and interior designers, advising mid-century homemakers to buy contemporary furniture and modern accessories that had been made specifically to complement the new architectural styles. Filling the home with new purchases had never been easier, as credit cards, store account facilities and low-interest loans offered easy payment terms. Free of the clutter of past lives and the furniture of outdated eras, mid-century home-owners took minimalism as their starting point. They began to decorate their homes by beginning with the architectural structure and then working inwards from there.

The type of simplicity advocated by architects and interior designers presented minimalism as a new prototype for living, which reconciled utility with the need for comfort and style. Despite their belief that form should follow function, designers and architects balanced luxury with practicality in styles that were economical and easy to maintain. The architecture and interior décor of the mid-century home were designed as a unified whole that could adjust easily to daily changes.

The sophisticated simplicity of the new architecture was intended to create an atmosphere of tranquillity in the home, since this was seen as being more conducive to an unwavering, methodical mindset than the unsettling effect of living among clutter and chaos. Nevertheless, many homes also found space for brilliant hues, rich textures and lavish motifs, combining the minimalism of the architecture with a wide variety of stylish patterns and colourful designs.

The 'new' minimalism had actually been introduced in the late 1920s by modernists such as Le Corbusier, Gropius and Mies van der Rohe. Although their functionalistic style had impact, it was not assimilated into mainstream interior design until 1950. Because the mid-century design idiom was partly inspired by the functionalistic style, many of the interiors bore a vague 1930s signature, which gave a retro dimension to mid-century décor. The modern interiors of the 1930s had been characterized by a machine aesthetic that juxtaposed undulating curves with symmetrical motifs and geometric repeats. Although wood and glass were the mainstays of the 1950s home, the understated ornamentation and shining metal finishes exuded 1930s style.

ABOVE The cool and understated look of many mid-century interiors was regarded as futuristic and forward-thinking.
RIGHT The shapely outlines of mid-century furniture, ceramics and art glass meant radical new forms, while zebra-skin rugs introduced dramatic textures into the home.

In the 1950s interior the visual effect of glossy chrome and polished steel pieces was intended to counteract their density. The leather and polished chrome of Mies van der Rohe's 1930s furniture designs were popular throughout the 1950s, as were pieces designed by Le Corbusier, René Herbst and Charlotte Perriand, and the ubiquitous tubular steel furniture designed by Marcel Breuer. Raymond Loewy injected chrome and Bakelite into the interior with his designs and also with the industrial forms he introduced during the decade. Born in France but a resident of the United States, Loewy translated a distinctly European sense of style into interior accessories and created a curvaceous but streamlined silhouette for household appliances.

The simple, sleek shapes that distinguished the mid-century interior also reflected the minimalist forms of sculptors such as Henry Moore, Constantin Brancusi and Barbara Hepworth, and the linear abstractions of sculptors like Alexander Calder.

ABOVE The streamlined modernism advocated by Mies van der Rohe had great impact on the mid-century interior. Farnsworth House, completed in 1951, redefined the home in terms of light, space and transparency. Walls were reduced to glass panels and surfaces were crafted in planes of sleek wood.

Minimalism in art revealed the power of restraint in aesthetics, and made the public aware that the more that was taken away, the more there was to see.

The minimalist designer and architect Greta Magnusson Grossman brought Scandinavian chic to the homes of many Americans during the 1950s. Grossman had emigrated to California from Sweden in the late 1930s, taking with her a highly individual approach to Swedish modernism, which went on to influence the California Modern style that eventually characterized modern West Coast homes of the 1950s. Without sacrificing her minimalist beliefs, she was able to accommodate traditional family heirlooms and classical antiques in her interiors, typically making features of them rather than attempting to integrate them fully in the overall decorating scheme. Grossman was unique in her appreciation of enduring designs, and many of her own interiors look timeless today.

ABOVE Comfort was essential to mid-century home-owners, who decorated their homes with overstuffed sprung furniture and tufted wool carpets to offset the austerity of the interior architecture. Natural textures, plus flowers and plants, gave the home a warm, inviting feel.

A fellow minimalist and an associate of Grossman, Milo Baughman helped create the California Modern look through simple, understated interiors featuring walnut, Formica and wrought iron. His restrained interiors were synonymous with the casual, open-plan architecture that was so popular in California, and he developed ingenious ways to maximize space and divide areas without building walls. At the beginning of the decade, Baughman also ran his own custom-design shop with Olga Lee in Los Angeles; Lee designed the hand-printed fabrics, wallpaper, lamps and accessories that coordinated with Baughman's furniture designs. The acclaim that Baughman and Grossman received for their Beverly Hills and Bel Air interiors, together with the architecture of Richard Neutra and Craig Ellwood, established Los Angeles as the centre of mid-century style.

Marcel Breuer, the Hungarian-born and Bauhaus-trained American architect, designed and furnished more than seventy private houses in New England and on the East Coast. Masculine and unadorned, his interiors were premised on a high standard of materials and artistic élan highlighted by his minimalist oeuvre. Breuer was unique among his contemporaries in his preference for contrasting forms rather than coordinating shapes and textures. The careful arrangement of matching pieces or the use of furniture suites was anathema to him; Breuer made space for each item in the home to be appreciated for its individuality. Interpreting a surface as an overriding minimalistic device, he would typically display a single item or arrange a small cluster of objects in a manner that would enable them to be appreciated for their sculptural attributes. Visible interior brickwork was usually painted white, as was most of the panelling in the interior, allowing the eye to rest more easily on natural materials or gaze upon artworks. Breuer eschewed cupboard doors in favour of sliding panels that disappeared altogether, and he often replaced exterior windows with sliding glass doors.

Mid-century styles of interior decoration were not strictly limited to architectural minimalism, however. Suspicion of contemporary architecture was paralleled by many people's dislike of modern interior schemes, and, subsequently, many retro styles were reintroduced. In the United States designs that mimicked eighteenth-century pieces or re-created the feel of the exotic East were popular, optimistically labelled Chinese Mandarin, Chippendale or French Provincial.

ABOVE 'Less is more' was a precept to which many mid-century home-owners adhered, and the practical aspects of minimalist style continue to prevail today. Limiting furnishings to a selection of key pieces makes a strong visual statement that can create a bold, masculine interior like the one pictured here.

RIGHT The minimalism of the 1990s had its roots in the 1950s, when the impact of bare surfaces, clean lines and dramatic shapes was first discovered by home-owners. Here, a glossy white dining table is framed by the sculptural contours of Verner Panton's plastic chairs, which offset the strict rectilinear shape. In the background the armchair and footstool from the Eames Aluminum Group create striking silhouettes, their black leather upholstery contrasting with the shiny white interior.

[The laid-back minimalism of many mid-century homes heralded the space-age craze for the futuristic interiors and forward-thinking furniture of the following decade.]

RIGHT Contrasting colours, abstract fabric motifs, vibrant artworks and colourful lighting characterize the mid-century interior, where they were typically combined in a nonchalant fashion. Today, the most expressive elements of 1950s décor can be juxtaposed to create an interior with real impact.

The Early American decorating style made its debut at this time, in designs that featured little decorative elaboration and made vague connections to America's colonial past. The simplified forms and rustic shapes recalled America's Shaker heritage and were popular among homemakers who appreciated traditional styles. A successful marriage of mass-produced pieces and rustic materials, Early American décor was usually commingled with vernacular pieces, and sometimes accentuated by cowhides, wagon wheels, terracotta pots and other icons of rural life, as well as much Americana.

Among the most maximalist decorative motifs in the Unites States was the theme of the circus and fairground, sketched out in pink, canary yellow, lime green and bright red. From the late 1940s through the mid-1950s, striped tents, carousel horses, performing animals and even figurative characters such as the Ringmaster, the Lion Tamer and the harlequin Acrobat featured on wallpaper, Formica and textiles. European gypsies were also heavily romanticized, and colourful images of caravans, open wagons, dancing girls and soothsayers were found on wallpaper and textile prints during the period. Circuses and gypsies preceded the lively folk art and handicraft motifs that became popular during the second half of the decade.

Based in Detroit, the architect-designer Alexander Girard used a rich colour palette, but tended to move away from the classic primary hues towards bright pinks or brilliant magentas. Girard's sense of style was shocking and exciting. In vivid contrast to the minimalism and restraint espoused by his colleagues, he disguised the stark outlines of contemporary furniture with lavish textile motifs and stylized patterns, and used decorative cladding to give them a colourful backdrop. Combining metal and coloured plastics, his designs all possessed a distinctive tactile quality. Girard also used the handicraft traditions of developing countries such as India and Mexico, enabling his work to become a vibrant counterpoint to American modernist furniture.

Another architect-designer, the Austrian Josef Frank began designing furniture for the Stockholm interior design company Svenskt Tenn in 1932, and eventually emigrated to Sweden before spending the war years in New York. Despite the modernism advocated by his colleagues in Vienna and Stockholm, for much of his life Frank remained true to the traditional Biedermeier idea that the home should be a haven for leisure and luxury rather than a place of efficiency and practicality. While his works were based on a purity of form that captured the essence of Nordic modernism, they were given a luxurious feel by exquisite motifs and impeccable craftsmanship.

Although Frank was renowned for his textile and furniture designs, he was also an architect. Realizing that interior design could express more about a home than the architecture could, he considered various methods of fully integrating textile design and interior decoration, effectively 'wallpapering' the architecture in order to create uniform looks. Frank's interior design schemes rarely included solid structural walls. Instead, he often deployed sumptuous draperies and panels of colourful fabric to divide spaces and make separate living areas, and these, in turn, complemented the lavish designs of his upholstery fabrics.

Frank regarded comfort as essential, and many of his signature pieces were epic in scale and overstuffed to the point of bursting. He gave his interiors a warm, inviting mood by including a living element in the form of potted plants, bowls of fruit and vases of flowers, and he contrasted clashing textiles to avoid the generic monochromatic décor advocated by many modernists. Recognizing the strong visual impact of his furniture designs and textile motifs, Frank advocated simple white walls as the best background for his domestic interiors. For embassies, state residences and hotels, however, he believed that the use of wallpaper was necessary, in order to maximize the effect of his décor on those who could visit only for a short time.

BELOW The 1950s is often associated with kitsch, and many of the period's eclectic range of designs are favourites of collectors of kitsch today. Flying ducks, sunburst clocks, animal-print fabrics and fake-fur rugs provide fun features for a lively contemporary interior, which can be dramatically offset by a background of vivid colours, as here.

LEFT Mid-century motifs are a source of inspiration for many contemporary wallpaper patterns, lining the walls of chic interiors with geometric repeats and colourful abstractions. Minimalist patterns such as Sven Markelius's Prisma (1958) and Arne Jacobsen's Trapeze (1949) inspired geometric wallpaper repeats, while American designers were known for their elegant line drawings and abstractions of household objects.

TOP RIGHT These autumnal leaves originally featured in a fabric designed by Margaret Hildebrand, a variation of her classic Empel pattern from 1950. The organic shapes of the 1940s gave way to the wavy biomorphic forms of the 1950s, which appeared in wallpaper designs just as they did in ceramics, glass and furniture.

TOP FAR RIGHT African motifs were popular among Scandinavian designers in the first years of the 1950s, inspiring wallpaper designs, like this one, that captured the spirit of the Congo. As exhibitions of African art began touring Norway and Denmark at the beginning of the decade, they made a strong impression on designers in all five Nordic nations.

BOTTOM RIGHT AND BOTTOM FAR RIGHT Diamond shapes and flattened roundels featured in many 1950s patterns. The verdigris tints and shadowed planes in this swatch of British wallpaper, reintroduced in 2004, have rich textural appeal. The soft shades and the regular shapes expressed the modernist mood of the decade and marked a sharp departure from the decorative art style that preceded it.

[Mid-century motifs possessed depth, a sense of movement and a distinctive textural richness. Walls were covered in vibrant lines and striking colours that brought these two-dimensional surfaces to life.]

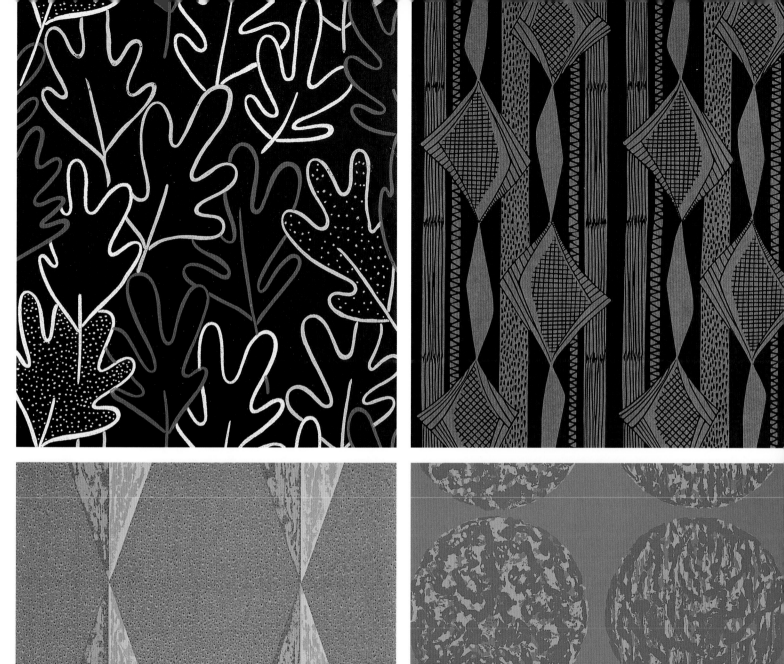
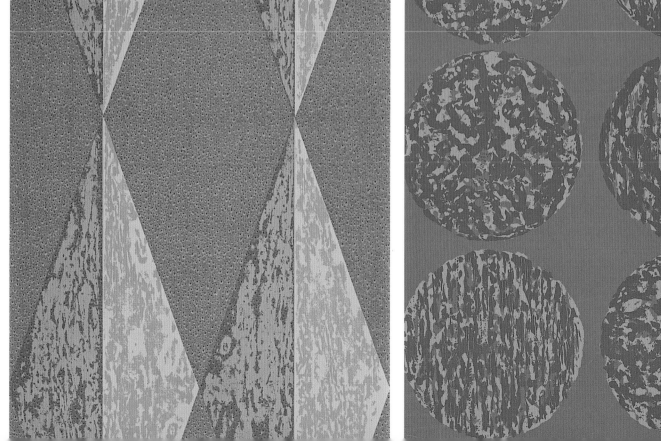

Materials

Although modern living was seen as a break with tradition, many time-honoured materials continued to define and enhance contemporary spaces. The use of wood and stone may have been rooted in the past, but they found renewed expression in the mid-century interior. Because these natural materials were preserved in 1950s interior architecture, their presence in the home re-established its links to the landscape around it. With wood grains, stone surfaces and vast windows revealing the sky, sunlight, trees and the earth as sources of inspiration, they integrated the home into nature.

The beauty and versatility of wood made it a favourite of architects and interior designers alike. The sensuous textures, subtle colours and fine grains that give wood a unique beauty were thought to surpass the merits of other materials. As a medium, wood was equated with permanence, because it was as durable and long-lasting as it was practical and good-looking. Wood trim was burnished to a dazzling shine and used to lift the architectural features of the rooms.

Stone flooring was typical of many mid-century interiors, particularly in North America. The dense, irregular shapes of flagstones provided a tough surface that was suitable for living rooms as well as for the terrace outside, helping to unify the two areas. Slabs of granite, squares of marble, ceramic tiles or glass bricks were polished to a high sheen and laid with geometric precision throughout the house, while terrazzo – an aggregate of coloured marble, granite pebbles and crushed glass – was poured in place to give a seamless finish. Simple blocks of polished marble, or mosaics laid out in ceramic or glass, were as popular in the Mediterranean in the 1950s as they are today, thanks to their cooling effects in warm weather.

The dense textures and repeated patterns of the stone floor were mirrored in interior cross walls constructed in the same materials. The rough, irregular surface of the flagstones that were used for the flooring acted as a foil for the smooth stones chosen to line the fireplace and hearth.

An open hearth, usually situated near the centre of a cross wall, radiated warmth and cast a flickering glow throughout the room. Chimney breasts were not built; the flue was constructed within the cross wall and hidden from view, with only the opening to reveal that it was a fireplace. Open-sided, pot-bellied cast-iron fireplaces were also

LEFT Panelling and plywood work together to create a streamlined kitchen in a home dominated by wood tones, with splashes of colour accenting an otherwise unadorned interior.
ABOVE RIGHT The rich sheen of the stone floor contrasts with the pale wood overhead. These distinctive textures continue to characterize mid-century style today.

popular, as were free-standing minimalist steel hearths. Their bulbous shapes were typically designed as one single, rounded sweep of metal that countered the rectilinear shapes of the interior architecture with smooth curves.

Mid-century architects regarded the ceiling as the fifth wall and designed it to communicate seamlessly with the rest of the interior. Case Study-style architecture (see page 18) featured exposed beams in the open-plan area, producing a rhythmic cadence across the ceiling. The beams supported a ceiling of varnished timber planks, which created a stunning, yet simple, wooden canopy overhead. Panelled ceilings were a feature of many mid-century architectural styles, especially those popular on America's West Coast and in Scandinavia.

The juxtaposition of wood and stone in the interior emphasized the rich patinas and dense textures of each. The heaviness of the stone flooring contrasted with the apparent weightlessness of the smooth wood lining the walls and the ceilings, and introduced a masculine tone. Dark hardwoods such as teak, mahogany, oak and wenge had great impact when polished; they provided a rich, glossy texture that complemented areas of bold colour or contrasted dramatically with pale surfaces.

ABOVE LEFT The exposed support beams and visible structural materials of 1950s architecture fore-shadowed the architecture of the 1990s.

ABOVE The mid-century home often combined industrial materials with natural textures. Here an exposed breeze-block wall is juxtaposed with cork flooring. The pine panelling on the ceiling mixes machine-like symmetry with organic textures.

THIS PAGE Red bricks, glazed ceramic tiles and unpolished stone come together in this robust fireplace, where they charge the home with dense, earthy elements. The irregular arrangement of the roughly cut stones sets up a vertical rhythm of organic textures and uneven shapes, balanced by the planes of wood in the rest of the interior.

[The choice of architectural materials was strongly rooted in the natural world, with wood, stone and clay tiles used in many mid-century homes. Elements from the landscape brought the beauty of nature indoors.]

Traditional wall panelling was crafted in pine, cedar, teak, oak and redwood to enhance the interior with subtle textures and natural finishes. Broad planks of solid wood clad the interior in wide panels, and the recessed joins between them created a vertical rhythm of parallel lines. Specialist interiors sometimes featured panelling in cherry or elm to add a note of luxury. The reddish-pink tinge of cherry gave the panelling a subtle, warm tint, while elm's dense, interlocking grain was greyish-white to light brown in tone and imparted a contrasting pattern of dark lines against a light background.

On America's West Coast, California's own redwood forests provided the dense, rosy-hued wood that was not only strong enough to support a house's structure but also beautiful enough to line the interior. Cedar, with its reddish grain and aromatic fragrance, held a similar appeal. Nordic pines, with their fine, smooth textures and polished surfaces, were widely used in Scandinavia and exported abroad. Oak could often be sourced from local forests in Europe and North America, where it was worked to a shimmering finish and crafted into flooring and other durable fixtures subjected to constant use. Architects throughout Europe and the United States used tropical hardwoods such as mahogany and wenge imported from the Far East, and teak was also a favourite. Previously associated more with luxury than functionality, teak was virtually the hallmark of the Danish Modern style during the 1950s.

Wood veneers were also popular in the interior, planed from expensive, elaborately patterned wood and expertly joined to a thicker, industrial sheet beneath them. Veneers were typically finished with a lustrous sheen achieved through repeated applications of a mixture of oils and lacquer, which were buffed entirely by hand and rarely subjected to further embellishment.

ABOVE LEFT Broad slabs of rosewood were used to construct this open-tread staircase, which makes a bold, minimalist statement. The supporting joist remains in view, showcasing the beauty of wood as well as craftsmanship techniques.
LEFT Panelled ceilings and walls were popular in mid-century homes. The unpainted surfaces of wide wooden planks were polished to a high sheen and covered the walls in natural patterns.

LEFT Architecture, soft furnishings and furniture effortlessly unite in this spectacular mid-century British house, which features a sunken den that fits in very well with the split-level arrangement. Leather upholstery, tufted rugs and textured curtains soften the hard surfaces of the construction materials and supply a visual link between the different levels.

Plywood, an industrially bonded wood aggregate, provided smooth, pale-toned, seamless veneers that could be either varnished or stained darker colours. A versatile material, it could be crafted into cupboard doors or built-in wardrobes and used for decorative cladding. Plywood and panelling were frequently used together to form a streamlined interior dominated by wood tones, perhaps in a kitchen constructed with plywood units, above which the ceiling would be lined with pine panelling. Irrespective of their different grains, all woods spoke a common language of simplicity and beauty that was seen as comfortable and inviting.

Although the mid-century architectural style was strongly rooted in the natural world, vinyl, linoleum, Formica and plastic linked the interior firmly to the man-made environment as well. Colourful vinyl or linoleum flooring was decorative and functional, providing clean, waterproof surfaces for the bathroom, kitchen and other high-traffic areas. Today manufacturers throughout the world are reintroducing classic vinyl sheet flooring and vinyl floor tiles in colours and designs that have a distinct mid-century signature. Although many new materials have been launched since the 1950s, the appeal of glossy vinyl has never waned. Formica, a hard, durable, plastic laminate, is easily moulded into thin panels of exceptional strength. Because its colour and motifs are part of its thin structure rather than just a veneer, its decorations

never fade or need to be renewed. Formica lined the countertops and cupboard doors of many mid-century kitchens, and it was also used for table surfaces by furniture manufacturers. Secured by adhesive or stainless-steel grips and sometimes embellished with chrome trim, Formica could be used to create a coordinated look for a kitchen as it linked the vertical and horizontal surfaces, and even the kitchen table.

Panels of glass maintained a strong presence in the mid-century interior, providing transparent screens and room dividers, as well as plate-glass windows that looked out onto the landscape. Because new developments in glass technology allowed it to be strengthened and reinforced, it could be pressed into larger panels than ever before. Durable enough to be held upright in a metal frame without additional supports, it could be mounted on tracks to construct sliding glass doors, which ingeniously combined a window with a space-saving door.

Picture windows channelled sunshine into the home and made the living space seem larger, while glass doors within the home also facilitated the passage of light. These internal glass doors, along with glass walls, reduced the noise level associated with open-plan spaces, while at the same time affording a direct visual connection. The use of transparency as a decorative theme was typical of the mid-century interior, where it created a stronger sense of continuity. Although glass walls and interior doors had featured in luxurious homes in the 1920s and '30s, they had typically been crafted in individual panels supported by heavy metal trim, hung awkwardly on iron hinges and opened with robust handles. But by the 1950s plate-glass features had become virtually a necessity rather than a luxury and were regarded as beautiful space-saving devices.

Today, as architects introduce new concepts of modern dwellings, their ideals continue to unfold through the use of glass panels, natural materials and the sort of plastics that were popular among mid-century homemakers. Whereas styles and techniques have changed radically over the years, the appreciation of these materials has not, and craftsmen continue to value them in contemporary homes.

ABOVE Plate-glass windows and doors channel natural light into this bedroom, allowing sunshine to stream in through transparent walls so that the garden seems to be an extension of the interior. The floor was crafted in light-coloured stone to reflect daylight across its polished surface.

RIGHT Mid-century dining areas known as breakfast nooks were often planned as part of the interior architecture. Custom-designed by Lee Froebel, this low banquette is upholstered in vinyl and replaces a suite of chairs with sofa-like seating. The banquette surrounds a classic Eames table.

Colour

Although the natural textures, pale tints and rich wood grains of the interior architecture created a palette of gentle earth tones in the mid-century home, richer colour nevertheless played a leading role. Whether overstated in sweeping surfaces or added sparingly in accents, bold colours were used to dazzle, highlight, unify and divide. Many vivid colour schemes were introduced during the 1950s, deposing the drab tones found in the wartime interiors of the previous decade.

Confident primary colours were employed to enliven the interiors of the time, but they did so without adding busyness, thereby remaining true to the modernist principle of minimalism. Monochrome colours covered surfaces in a single vibrant sweep, satisfying the eye without subjecting it to a wide range of ornamentation. Blocks of colours maximized the contrast between painted surfaces and natural textures, intensifying their effect on the interior. Mid-century homes may have been smaller than those of previous decades, yet they were designed to be roomy and uncluttered, and accents of strong hues counteracted the sense of emptiness that bare space could evoke. In fact, the psychological effects of colour in the interior were quantified by scientific research that was conducted during the 1950s. Noting that colour preferences came from feeling as much as from observation, psychologists charted colour's subtle influence on mood and behaviour and reported their findings. Dusty pastels were thought to produce an atmosphere of harmony within the interior, while dark, dull, matt colours were believed to generate a sense of relaxation and tranquillity. Consequently, muted, lacklustre colours such as taupe, dark grey and chocolate brown were sometimes used to decorate quiet areas of the home.

Deep primary pigments, such as dark reds and deep greens, tended to moderate the passage of light and could therefore have created a dense, enclosed mood, but the open spaces and easy transmission of light in the contemporary interior ensured that the colours rarely seemed oppressive.

FAR LEFT The variety of vibrant hues on these cupboards and drawers provide a colourful antidote to the strict functionalism of the cabinets. In the 1950s, appliances, too, were manufactured in a range of colours to enhance their decorative appeal.
LEFT The bold primary colours of Charlotte Perriand's steel and wood bookcase gave it a strong presence in the mid-century home. Used today as a dining sideboard in this home, its planes of rich colour coordinate with the red upholstery of the dining chairs.
ABOVE A detail of an oak desk attributed to Finn Juhl highlights the exuberant veneers of laminated plastic he used to enhance the drawers.

LEFT The mid-century interior transformed the colourless modernist interiors of the 1930s and '40s using a colour palette that ranged from bright hues through earth tones to so-called neutral shades. The walls, textiles, ceramics and decorative accents of this contemporary home were taken from the earth tones that were popular during the 1950s.

Vivid colours, on the other hand, were thought to be stimulating and revitalizing. Hues such as lime green, tangerine, scarlet and canary yellow adorned the television room, games room or other entertainment spaces. These also made up the palette of the classic American diner, whose bubblegum colours and neon signs were intended to energize their clients. The scale of motifs used to decorate the home was thought to be significant and was believed to have a similar effect; large, bold designs were enlivening and exciting, while small repeats were restful and even soothing.

Colours were much more distinct in the early 1950s than in the ranges available today – in the 1950s, most decorators created unique colour schemes rather than shopping for premixed paints. This convention changed dramatically as the decade wore on;

manufacturers devised unique colour palettes for their appliances and required homemakers to choose from a variety of new enamel shades. Despite the efforts of organizations that had attempted for several decades to standardize colour names in their dictionaries and source books, new colour charts were introduced faster than they could be recorded. Tones like blue-green and red-orange, for example, were given names such as sea green, leaf green, sunset and ginger. Many homemakers were baffled by the new colour palettes in which the names of foods and beverages featured. Few could agree on the colours of 'coffee', 'citrus' or 'biscuit'; and while 'cinnamon' was easy to grasp, the precise tone of 'champagne' was heavily disputed.

Much of colour's visual effect depends upon the quality of light in the interior, and so the 'temperature' (warmth or coolness) of ambient light was used to determine the colours used or was harnessed as a means of enhancing a colour scheme. Brilliant, jewel-like colours have mirror-like properties that aid the transmission of light through a room, giving a lustrous sheen that reflects across other surfaces. Luminous colours like these remain visible even when seen in a darkened room, continuing to have visual impact after the lighting level is lowered. Colours, therefore, were never chosen by shade alone for the mid-century interior; a surface was deliberately painted light or dark in tone, shiny or matt, to absorb or reflect light.

The beauty of decorating with bright colours is that they appear to radiate light from beneath their surface, so long as the diffused lighting and direct lighting in the room are properly balanced. When diffused light is directed over a coloured surface, it creates the iridescent hues of a Mark Rothko canvas. Colour experts of the 1950s favoured tones that they considered to be the most light-reflective, and grouped colours together that would both give out and reflect light. Blue and yellow, for example, were often paired to maximize their individual effects – yellow seemed more luminous when juxtaposed with blue than with other colours, and blue seemed to take on iridescent properties when yellow was placed beside it.

The growing popularity of contemporary art injected the shocking pastels, yellow ochres and deep primary colours of the abstract expressionists' palette into the core of the home. Whether presented on large-scale canvases or reproduced in the many prints and lithographs of the decade, paintings added a feeling of vitality to the interior's colour schemes. Wall murals boldly painted in rich colours, or mosaics painstakingly created in glass or ceramic, supplied vibrant backdrops and set the tone of the décor.

Colours that were used together in 1950s interiors were not necessarily the sharply contrasting ones that are opposite each other on the colour wheel (a designer's device in which the colours are arranged in a circle, in the same order in which they appear in the spectrum). Some decorators preferred analogous colours, which lie near each other

BELOW From the muddy shade of the chocolate-coloured walls and the soft textures of the tawny carpet to the golden tones of the rosewood bedstead, earth colours form an inviting interior landscape in this bedroom. The silvery grey of the bedspread and the greenish grey of the cushion sharpen up the room's natural tones with a metallic sheen.

[The vibrant abstractions and colourful décor of the 1950s interior foreshadowed the op art and pop art of the 1960s. Psychedelia and Flower Power broke free from geometric repeats and muted tones.]

on the colour wheel, such as red, yellow and orange. As these colours were interspersed throughout the interior, they formed a grid of rich colour over a living area. With colourful linoleum-topped surfaces, for example, tables, sideboards and free-standing screens furnished the home with blocks of colour. The use of such surfaces was usually deployed as a decorative device throughout rather than being restricted to just one or two pieces. An interior may have had, say, a royal-blue surface on the dining table, which would have contrasted with the canary-yellow surface of the adjacent sideboard. Horizontal panels of orange linoleum could have been hung flush against the wall, perhaps forming a backdrop for wall heaters or home appliances, or functioning as a cupboard door. Combined with wood furniture and other organic elements, the coloured surfaces would set off the natural materials, emphasizing their textures.

Widely popular in the 1950s, the harlequin colour palette consisted of a rainbow of bright tones used for appliances, flooring, accessories and textiles, even becoming popular as paint colours for exteriors. Harlequin hues seemed to legitimize the use of bright colours and made it fashionable to combine a broader range than ever before, even making it acceptable to 'clash' colours. The harlequin palette revelled in some of the vibrant combinations that were preferred by the abstract expressionists, and which were also present in the patterns and motifs inspired by their artworks.

The coordination of colour schemes and patterns created a market for interior textiles to match wallpaper. The repeated motifs that appeared on the fabrics were also used on matching wallpapers, and popular patterns could even be found on the surfaces of plastic laminates, ceramics and interior cladding. The new biomorphic forms (see page 92) used in shapes and motifs required a vivid colour palette in order to make them

RIGHT Bold, colourful wall motifs like these introduced a strong graphic signature to the modern home that superseded traditional wall murals or conventional patterned wallpaper. Overlapping colours were used to suggest movement, while ochre tones generated a sense of warmth and vitality. The blue club chairs were designed by Jens Risom.

more dynamic. Panel prints of botanical motifs designed by Vanderborght Frères in Belgium incorporated plants in lurid colours to give them a surrealistic aura. They were combined with fabrics containing the same motifs.

During the 1950s white was considered to be a classic colour rather than a contemporary one. By then, the stark white, clinical interior of the functionalist era had lost its appeal as a stylistic extreme. White was associated with lightness and brilliance, sunshine, luminosity and candlelight. Walls painted in eggshell, ivory, cream and off-white gave the interior a crisp, clean feeling without the sobering, antiseptic associations that are sometimes assigned to white today. The American designer Edward Wormley is remembered for the white walls and light-coloured flooring of his showrooms and interior design schemes. He contrasted the black outlines of his dark mahogany furniture against the pale background, as if framing the dynamic upholstery textiles he used against a white gallery wall.

Combinations of white and pastel colours created a cool mood in the contemporary interior. The pastel shades known as Bermuda pink, spring green, fern green, dawn grey, sandy beige, buttercup yellow, harvest yellow and lagoon blue were introduced in the mid-1950s. Lacking the visual intensity of bold colours, pastels were regarded as conducive to relaxation and warmth. Because they could easily fade into the background, they were believed to generate an illusion of space, making walls seem to recede and rooms appear more spacious.

The concept of what constitutes a neutral colour has changed dramatically since the mid-twentieth century. Back then, neutral colours were limited to black, white and grey – they did not include the earth tones of beige, off-white and buff that we think of as neutral today. Black and white became a popular colour combination through the dramatic tension between them, as seen in the black-and-white chequerboard flooring often found in mid-century kitchens and bathrooms.

Many of the colourful abstractions that characterized the mid-century home foreshadowed the psychedelia and 'hippy' colours of the following decade, while others were revived in the Italian designer Ettore Sottsass's Memphis style of the 1980s. As today's designers revisit the timeless interiors of the 1950s, both the daring colour schemes and the muted tones of the decade find renewed expression in the twenty-first century, attesting to the enduring appeal of the mid-century palette.

LEFT Buttercup yellow was a signature colour of the 1950s and very popular in kitchens, where it was used for appliances, worktops, flooring or wallpaper. **ABOVE** Many new paint colour charts containing intermediate tones were introduced in the 1950s. Here, the walls have been painted to match the subtle shade of the wool upholstery on these fibreglass Eames chairs.

Soft furnishings

ABOVE Lucienne Day
pioneered abstract textile
designs. Her Calyx print,
shown here, introduced
new colour combinations
and initiated a move away
from traditional repeating
patterns when it was
designed in 1951.
RIGHT Mid-century
textiles look remarkably
contemporary right now,
whether used as part
of a brand-new interior
or to re-create a 1950s
mood. The cushion covers
shown here are made in
fabric designed in 1952
by the Viennese designer
Jacqueline Groag.

For the first half of the twentieth century, textile artists had been restricted to designing muted patterns and pastoral prints that would appeal to the masses. This changed radically in the 1950s, when textile design gained a reputation for innovation and individuality, and forged an important link between art and design. Fabrics and ready-made ranges of bed linen, table linen and curtains were produced in playful patterns and traditional folk-art motifs, or in high-design expressions reflecting movements in painting, sculpture, graphics and even architecture. Using a spare vocabulary of classic shapes, natural earth tones and primary colours, textile designers created breathtakingly simple designs that took minimalism to a higher level.

The sensuous appeal of fabrics was such that leading furniture designers like Gio Ponti, Arne Jacobsen and Terence Conran also dabbled in textile design. Jacobsen's Trapeze design (pictured on page 44) united four contrasting colours in interlocking triangular repeats, while Ponti's Sticks motif printed alternating green, yellow and black lines on heavy cotton Flamenco fabric. Many of Conran's screen-printed fabrics featured graphic motifs in black and white against vibrant primary-coloured backgrounds.

The British boast a long tradition of stylized fabrics, but at the onset of the 1950s designers and the government-funded Council of Industrial Design came together to shake off historical influences and move textile design forward. The Council encouraged designers to take inspiration from geometric patterns based on natural crystals in an attempt to foster a rapport between science and art. When the Festival of Britain opened in 1951, the works of many visionary young designers were showcased.

Calyx, a screen-printed linen fabric designed by Lucienne Day, wife of the furniture designer Robin Day, won international acclaim as a result of being exhibited at the Festival. Calyx was manufactured by Heal's Fabrics, which subsequently commissioned Day to produce up to six designs annually for its textile collections. Day's success is attributed to the bold originality of her designs, which bridged the gap between traditional tastes and avant-garde style. Her designs moved away from the grid-like regularity of many of her contemporaries' textiles towards random abstractions or simple graphic lines outlined against a dark surface. Flotilla, introduced in 1952, suggested bright-coloured buoys floating in a painterly sea of rolling waves, while Quadrille revealed Day's talent for linear abstractions.

Day did not work in isolation, but considered the way her designs would interact with other interior elements. Experimenting with designs that would suit the dimensions of modest-sized homes, she avoided creating overpowering areas within the confines of a domestic interior. Although Calyx featured large-scale motifs, it worked well within a modest room, and smaller repeats such as the rhythmic Springboard and Highway patterns provided focal points for the eye that suited a room of any size.

By the middle of the decade, Day was finding inspiration from other areas of design. Patterns like Lapis and Isosceles reflected contemporary architecture in their overlying motifs and contrasting planes. Day also united the separate genres of fashion and soft furnishings through her colour palettes and design idiom. In 1954 she designed six dress fabrics for Cavendish Textiles, some of which drew on her motifs for interior fabrics; and she based a colour chart for household textiles on the fashion colours of the preceding season. Day's work extended to include carpets and wallpapers, and commissions from abroad eventually established her as a designer of international repute.

In the Nordic countries, where refined fibres were often in short supply, interior fabrics were highly decorative and were generally regarded as the height of luxury. Textile design had been acknowledged as a fine art for several centuries, and many designers studied fine art before accepting an apprenticeship as a weaver.

ABOVE LEFT Bluebells, lily of the valley and periwinkles, loved for their delicate blossoms and elfin shapes, were revived during the 1950s in prints such as G P & J Baker's Harebell, pictured here.

ABOVE This Pillar fabric, which was screen-printed onto linen, is painterly in its wavy repeats. The design was produced by the London design studio Silver Studio in 1933 and remained in production throughout the 1950s.

Lis Ahlmann, a renowned textile artist from Denmark, originally studied painting before becoming distinguished for her textile designs. The simple parallel stripes, checked patterns and organic abstractions that Ahlmann designed took shape in a muted palette of coppery browns, yellow ochres, olive greens and antique white. Many of her textiles featured in the Design in Scandinavia exhibition that toured North America in the 1950s. The popularity of her work made her one of the key designers responsible for the post-war renaissance in Scandinavian textiles, and her work sparked the craze for minimalist textiles that accompanied the Danish Modern movement.

In Sweden works by textile artists such as Elsa Gullberg, Astrid Sampe, Dagmar Lodén and Josef Frank are acknowledged as design classics today. Gullberg and Sampe had both designed textiles for industrial production, decorated in vibrant primary colours and abstract repeats. During the war years, when raw materials and export orders were scarce, Gullberg revitalized the hand-weaving tradition. Once she was able to resume production of her screen-printed rayon textiles, she designed a wide range of interior fabrics popular in the 1950s. Astrid Sampe was known for more minimalist designs, such as her linear Termidor motif in black and white, printed against shades of canary yellow, ochre and daffodil.

Dagmar Lodén's dynamic Thistles textile of 1949 was popular throughout the 1950s and is still in production today. Traditionally thistles were depicted as docile flowers, but she rendered them as menacing, jagged barbs and thorny stems against bold backgrounds of crimson or dark blue. Her signature style featured jagged lines and pointed shapes. Whereas nature was traditionally sweetened and made more romantic in most Swedish textile motifs, Lodén's representation of predatory plant life created a witty reversal of the natural world.

Josef Frank's textile designs span his entire career as a furniture designer and an architect (see page 43). Even before he moved to Sweden to design for the interior design company Svenskt Tenn, Frank had produced an extensive range of interior textiles in Vienna. Many of his iconic textiles were designed in the 1940s and produced after the war, becoming popular in the luxury homes of Scandinavia and the United States during the 1950s. Throughout his career, he was fascinated by the exotic vegetation flourishing beyond the borders of Europe, exploring it with surreal fascination. In his Himalaya textile, designed in 1950, Frank

BELOW Many 1950s textile designs are making a comeback today as stunning accents for the contemporary home. In this bedroom decorated with mid-century furniture and fabrics, the simple Eames Dots pattern is coordinated with unadorned bed linen from today's designers.

downscaled the mountain peaks into soft mounds overgrown with calla lilies, orchids, daisies and fruits. Another textile, Brazil, is a vibrant fusion of succulent fruits, blossoming flowers and serpentine creepers, while Tehran is a cornucopia of foliage, red branches, looping vines and sprays of blossom against a night sky.

Armed with North American field guides, Frank embarked on a quest to discover the plant life of America's Deep South and the deserts of the West. The Southern states grew fragrant magnolias and yielded ripe crops of watermelons, which Frank split open to capture the velvety pinkness of their flesh in his Dixieland design. His California print depicts nasturtium, sweet pea, dahlia and zinnia, which Frank 'planted' in a winding trail through the desert background. In Hawaii, he depicted purple trees with yellow branches, variegated flower petals and delicate butterflies.

Frank updated the ancient tree of life symbol in his Green Birds textile print. In it a flock of green birds – olive-coloured starlings, sea-green doves and jade-tinted parrots – gather on the branches of a flowering tree, while lithe herons and happy ducks paddle in a flowing stream beneath its roots. No less than 125 fabric patterns were printed during Frank's lifetime, and about forty are today textile classics, their bold and artistic patterns having ensured their survival long after the colours have begun to fade.

The Finnish textile designer Maija Isola was the first design director of Marimekko, the Finnish textile company. Isola had studied painting before joining the firm in 1949, where she transformed simple cotton sheeting into avant-garde patterns and bold abstractions. Isola's interior ranges brought vibrant motifs to every part of the household, in curtains and cushions as well as table napkins and place mats.

Her textiles for the early 1950s were inspired by African art, characterized by bright colours and unsteady, hand-painted stripes, as featured in her Lokki and Silkkikuikka motifs. By the mid-1950s she was decorating her fabrics with a range of floral motifs, before becoming influenced by Slovakian folk motifs towards the end of the decade. Isola gained acclaim in the United States in the Design in Scandinavia exhibition, eventually stimulating a market there for Marimekko textiles. Almost every one of Isola's mid-century fabric designs is regarded as a classic today, and many are even more popular now than when they were first manufactured in the 1950s.

One of the biggest North American names in mid-century textile design was Alexander Girard, mentioned earlier for his interior design schemes (see page 42). He created a number of textile patterns for the American furniture manufacturers Herman Miller. The company produced Girard's designs on screen-printed fabrics and wallpapers. At the time, fabrics were seen as functional rather than beautiful, but Girard revolutionized the look of the North American interior by making vivid colours, bold geometric patterns and overlapping graphic shapes integral to home textiles.

TOP RIGHT Josef Frank's Brazil textile design is even more popular today than it was in the 1950s. The flowing designs and strong colours evoke the lush flora of Brazil's exotic landscape.

TOP FAR RIGHT The Pohjanmaa fabric designed by Maija and Kristina Isola for Marimekko recalls a mosaic or stained-glass pattern as it draws the eye along its sloping lines and contrasting colours.

BOTTOM RIGHT Dagmar Lodén's Thistles textile of 1949 was considered daringly abstract, and it sparked a shift away from traditional floral motifs.

BOTTOM FAR RIGHT The terracotta urns surrounded by fig leaves and flower clusters in Maija and Kristina Isola's Amfora fabric reference Ancient Greece in bold freehand lines.

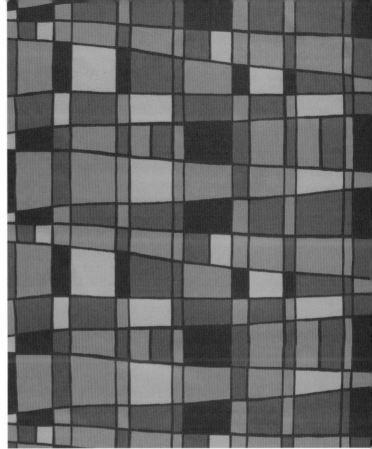

Lighting

Arne Jacobsen once remarked that 'light gives all things their presence', and his statement highlights the importance of ambient light in the interior and its capacity to yield dramatic effects. In fact, light was one of the defining characteristics of the 1950s home, as the drive to make houses lighter and brighter broke down the scale of exterior walls. The transparent doors, wide windows and angled ceilings adopted by mid-century architects were created to aid the passage of light throughout the home. They related the proportions and positions of windows to the scale of the interior to ensure that light travelled into the heart of the house. In open-plan areas this maximized the amount of ambient light, eliminating dark shadows and murky corners. As the light moved across the room through windows in opposite walls, it lent the interior a quality of weightlessness.

Light, both natural and artificial, played a critical role in the mid-century interior. Rooms were often lit from above by long pendant lamps, ceiling lamps or spotlights to re-create the brilliance of daylight at any time of day, while floor lamps, table lamps and wall lights were strategically positioned to take into account the same factors considered when artworks are lit in a gallery. The concept of diffused lighting became established in mainstream domestic interiors during the 1950s, introducing the idea of subdued, 'mood' lighting. The mechanics of lamps and spotlights also changed during the decade; the widespread use of swivel joints made for much greater flexibility in lighting, enabling the beams to be deflected or rotated by up to 360 degrees towards the area where light was needed.

Because the angle of a spotlight could be adjusted, it proved ideal for highlighting a painting or sculpture and also for directing light over a work surface. Mid-century spotlights were produced

RIGHT The Arredoluce three-arm floor lamp was a standard feature in many mid-century homes. Each arm was designed with a cylindrical handle that could be manipulated to adjust the angle of the light bulb, and each lamp could swivel up to 360 degrees to project the beam of light in any direction. Less versatile but equally inventive, 1950s ceramic table lamps balanced abstract form against functional use in designs that were both sculptural and practical.

[Lighting is as important as any architectural element – the amount of daylight allowed into a room can produce a stark intensity or a subdued atmosphere.]

in an amazing range of stylish designs that bore a distinct minimalist signature, often streamlined in a machine-like fixture that resembled an industrial component. The lights were generally crafted in metal, and the swivel bracket that mounted them on the ceiling was an integral part of the design. Spotlights were sometimes intended to be features in their own right, and usually were either crafted with shining chrome, copper or gilt finishes, or enamelled in a range of harlequin colours.

Most ceiling lights were designed with decorative paper or fabric shades, which were produced in a wide assortment of solid colours and were covered with a variety of motifs. In Britain, the lighting manufacturer W S Chrysaline's most popular designs were white, umbrella-like wire frames that were covered by a plastic-coated membrane embellished with gold stars. Other types of ceiling fitting had several arms emanating from a central axis which dispersed the beams in different directions. Typically, this variety would have had plastic-coated shades or enamelled reflectors tempering the bulbs.

Many ceiling lamps had shades made of glass, which had been etched, sandblasted or tinted to give an opaque finish that would conceal the bulbs. Most glass shades were produced in white, so that in British homes and in those of continental Europe they would coordinate more easily with white ceilings. The shades were flattened into soft contours in order to hug the ceiling more closely, often with edges that scrolled downwards or turned upwards towards the ceiling. The glass shells were mounted in place with chrome-plated caps that concealed the screws fastening them to the ceiling.

All-metal ceiling lamps generally echoed the shapes of glass shades and were usually fitted with louvres in the base to soften the beam of light. Lamps of this type resembled a rounded ventilation grille more than a light fixture. The metal shades were sometimes perforated with clusters of tiny circles or a small starburst shape that let the light shine through.

Pendant lamps either floated elegantly above the room or were lowered to eye level in order to light a surface or to have more impact. Simple pendants were for the most part round in

LEFT Poul Henningsen's PH-5 pendant lamp has not wavered in appeal since it was designed in 1957. The lamp was constructed with contouring blades of metal that could diffuse the light evenly without creating glare, and was admired by architects such as Mies van der Rohe and Alvar Aalto.

RIGHT Lighting triptychs were a hallmark of mid-century lighting, when pendant lights, table lamps and floor lamps often incorporated three separate light fixtures in a single design.

shape and were crafted in smooth glass that gave them the appearance of glowing orbs or were constructed from curving panels. Metal pendants typically had shades perforated into geometric cut-outs that counteracted their mass. These were lined with an inner shade of coloured fabric which hid the outline of the light bulb. Some of the most memorable pendants from the 1950s are the large-scale frames fitted with between four and twenty-two lamps. Their design positioned them somewhere between contemporary chandeliers and sculptural mobiles, and often the most elaborate of these were suspended from double-height ceilings.

Paper lantern shapes, like George Nelson's Bubble lamps, were widely popular, as were the white lanterns capped in brass that were produced by Ateljé Lyktan in Sweden. Silk fabrics were treated with plastic to make them flame-retardant and were then stretched over wire frames in virtually every curvaceous shape imaginable.

They still look appealingly current today, and their unwavering popularity could be attributed to their resemblance to the classical shapes that have been produced continuously in China for several thousand years.

Many of the mid-century lights that remain contemporary today were originally designed in Sweden, Denmark or Finland, where a number of models have been reintroduced or have been in continuous production since they were first manufactured. The dark days and long, cold nights of the Nordic winter made artificial light an essential part of the Scandinavian interior, and during the 1950s lighting was designed to become an instant focal point for any room. Danish designers often created lighting features more akin to cubist sculpture than conventional lamps: Poul Henningsen's complicated structures deployed several strata of overlapping blades, enabling strong light to cascade over a large area without blinding the eyes. Henningsen's Artichoke lamp and PH-Contrast lamp have been among the best-selling pendants in recent history. Louis Poulsen's elegant pendants often resembled futuristic jewellery more than lighting, while the stark, simple outlines of Arne Jacobsen's pendant shades recalled the curving shapes of Alexander Calder's sculptural mobiles.

Wall lights were designed in a range of shapes and silhouettes, including flat lampshades that fastened to the wall just as overhead lighting hugged the ceiling; arcing brackets that cantilevered over the floor, recalling the gesture of an arm holding a torch; and spotlight designs that swivelled on the wall to angle the light upwards or to the side. While their profiles recalled the torchères and sconces of the 1920s and '30s, their design idioms and use of materials were dramatically different. Wall lights could be further divided into two categories: lamps that projected light up towards the ceiling, where it could be reflected back into the room, and light fixtures that cast a beam inwards along the wall and diffused it with a shade angled downwards.

ABOVE LEFT The rooms in Copenhagen's iconic mid-century Royal Hotel which Arne Jacobsen designed were redecorated several decades later but recently 'updated' with many of his classic designs. Here, wall lights sit flush with the panelling, while a swivel spotlight has been added for bedtime reading.
ABOVE Poul Henningsen's Artichoke pendant is one of today's most popular mid-century designs.
RIGHT These lamps were designed by Achille Castiglione for Floss in 1954. Constructed from new membranes that were developed for the aero-space industry, they were made taut and translucent.

Lamps with upward beams were best suited to rooms with smooth white or pale-coloured ceilings rather than textured or panelled ones that would mottle the effect with shadows.

Design companies such as Stilnovo in Italy were leaders in innovation, producing wall lamps on extendable swivel arms fitted with pulleys that enabled a pendant shade to be adjusted to the desired height. Troughton & Young, in Britain, produced the Mondolite bracket light, a similar design in metal with a plastic shade that could be moved vertically and horizontally from its fixed position on the wall. The General Electric Company, also in Britain, created a version that dipped over the floor in an arc that suggested the angle of a modern London streetlight, fitted with a traditional shade made of pleated buckram.

Some of the most effective wall lamps designed in the 1950s had adjustable swivel joints that enabled them to hug the wall and project their beam along its surface, or be swivelled downwards and radiate their light up towards the ceiling. Several Stilnovo designs had such a feature, as did many wall lights that came from Finland and Denmark. Ateljé Lyktan produced rotating lamps crafted in brass or gilt-coloured metals, in which the brackets were integrated with the shade itself.

Decorative wall-light panels came into circulation during the 1950s, framing silhouettes of flowers, figures or abstractions against an illuminated background of white opaline glass. The motifs were cut out in hammered copper, matt chrome or tarnished silver, their stark outlines dramatically highlighted when the bulbs were switched on. The shadow-box effect this produced gave the wall panels an artistic dimension as it contrasted the profile of the motifs against the light background, yet also gave off a warm glow of soft light.

Table lamps were highly decorative during the 1950s, usually providing background lighting rather than serving as the main light source. Stoneware pottery lamps were a favourite, decorated with brush-work finishes and fitted with pleated fabric shades. Streamlined lamps had stems made of wood such as teak, cherry or mahogany, often with shades that had a deflector at the top to diffuse the light onto the surface below. Table lamps were

ABOVE Previously, floor lamps had been stationary designs with static fixtures, but in the 1950s they became interactive and adjustable. On this lamp the pivoting arm was fitted with a swivel joint enabling it to rotate 360 degrees, held in position by a counterweight.

sometimes combined with other objects: a telephone table might incorporate a stem lamp; or a desk set consisting of matching bookends, stationery boxes and pen holders would include a coordinating reading lamp as well.

A trend emerged for highly sculptural lamps that looked like expressionistic works or figurative abstractions. Most metalwork lamps mimicked Alberto Giacometti's attenuated sculptures or took the form of wavy abstractions, but the table lamps designed by Achille Castiglioni took both the medium and the material to a higher level. He experimented with the volume and proportions characteristic of traditional lamps, redefining their shapes in expressive contours set atop a marble base.

Ceramics and glass mirrored each other in the twisting, undulating profiles they assumed, both genres influenced by the biomorphic shapes that revolutionized mid-century furniture design. Coloured-glass or clear crystal bases were especially beautiful when they were illuminated. The French manufacturer Daum excelled at these, and its table lamps from the 1950s are highly prized by collectors today.

Many of the designers known for their table lamps were also acclaimed for their floor lamps. In France Serge Mouille used tubular steel and enamelled shades to make his distinctive tripod lamps, which he later scaled down to a miniature tabletop version. Throughout the 1950s Mouille designed large, angular, insect-like floor lamps with multiple arms, as well as smaller, curvaceous wall sconces. Some of his best-known designs from the period are his Oeil lamp of 1953, his Flammes design, produced the following year, and Saturn, designed in 1958. Mouille worked to achieve a sense of movement in space, creating a kinetic, sculptural aesthetic as a result.

The boundaries between floor lamps and other pieces of furniture became blurred during the 1950s, when a lamp might have been combined with a side table or console, or might have featured an extended ledge around the stem to function as a tabletop. Such innovations horrified the leading designers of the day, who were adamant that the two genres should remain distinct from each other. Yet designers of both would undoubtedly have agreed that noting where the light falls is a crucial consideration in placing and arranging furniture and decorative objects. Even though lighting is ephemeral, its impact cannot be overstated.

Mid-century
innovations went on to
shape subsequent lighting.
The sweeping arc of
Achille Castiglione's Arco
lamp is counterweighted
in a marble base, imitating
the curving stems of
Paul Laszlo's designs.
The Panthella table lamp
recalls the contours of
Saarinen's Tulip chairs, and
the shapes of Jacobsen's
enamelled shades.

FURNITURE

When the sleek furniture of the baby-boom generation's youth started appearing in antiques shops, it was not so much a sign of old age as a statement of style.

In the short period between the appearance of organic designs in 1940 and the pop-art revolution of 1960, designers produced some of the most significant furniture of the twentieth century. A number of classic pieces from the 1950s are hailed as timeless designs today, with many such modern classics and icons of the era now regarded as the next generation of antiques.

Mid-century furniture shrugged off the stylistic legacy of the art nouveau period and streamlined the bulky silhouettes that characterized art deco. Whereas these early twentieth-century styles had found expression in the interiors of their respective periods, mid-century modernists eschewed the notion that chairs, tables, sofas and cabinets should be designed strictly as interior accessories, and set out to redefine furniture as unique statements of design. Spurred on to produce furniture that could furnish the contemporary interior appropriately, they crafted simple pieces that had a resounding impact on their slick surroundings.

The new styles of furniture took centre stage with the distinctive shapes that continue to typify the look today. While mid-century furniture is often recognizable by its balance of form and function, its impact resulted from its ability to convey the dynamics of lived experience in static form. Mid-century designers regarded furniture as tactile art intended to cradle the human form. Although the use of new materials and techniques pioneered a change of direction for furniture – with moulded and glued plywood, and plastics reinforced by fibreglass, among the exciting developments – the forms continued to take shape in relation to the human body. Designers used furniture to articulate the tension between movement and stillness, which can never be separated from the human body. Consequently, 1950s furniture often expressed a body-consciousness unknown to other traditions.

Mid-century designers were determined to move beyond the perception of a chair merely as a functional object. Old-school furniture craftsmen believed that chairs required four legs and an imposing back to make them sturdy, which meant that they were too bulky to stow away in cupboards and were awkward to move easily. Chairs support certain points of the body while allowing ease of movement in others. As each chair is streamlined and perfected to strike a balance between form and functionality, it yields to the seated posture like a glove enveloping a hand. Mid-century designs were premised on innovation as much as on aesthetics, often employing ergonomic principles in order to craft the seat and back in a single piece of wood or merge the arms and legs into one visual gesture.

The new look of mid-century furniture reflected the international collaborations that were occurring between designers and manufacturers around the world. European designers such as Franco Albini, Marco Zanuso and Robin Day were known in the United States through their participation in design competitions, notably Organic Design in Home Furnishings in 1940 and the International Competition of Low-cost Furniture Design in 1948. The Dutch designer Cees Braakman travelled to the United States to seek out the work of Eero Saarinen and of Charles and Ray Eames as he pursued a new national style for The Netherlands. The furniture that was featured in the North American tour of the Design in Scandinavia exhibition in the mid-1950s redefined the work of many American designers, while the standardized proportions introduced by Mogens Koch in Denmark had an impact on furniture production worldwide. Koch pioneered the standardized height of chair seats, width of beds and depth of drawers. Guidelines such as these became the backbone of designs manufactured in multiples, and advanced the evolution of modular furniture.

The standardized sizes were reflected in virtually every type of furniture, contributing to the simplification of mass-market designs that had not previously reflected the new style. Certain types of mainstream furniture in the United States, and some styles of luxury furniture in Britain and France, were based on traditional styles that had been merely 'updated' with contemporary elements. American shopping malls and mail-order catalogues sold overstuffed sofas and chairs fashioned in the silhouettes of the 1930s and '40s, made without arms and designed in box-like, rectangular shapes, or crafted in organic contours. Lightweight cabinets were manufactured in wood veneer and the doors and drawers fitted with simple metal pulls or wooden handles. These were typically set atop splayed wooden legs or wiry metal ones attached with screws. In fact, most mainstream furniture reflected some innovations of high design, with wall-mounted clock faces, tilting headboards, office-style desks and modular units filtering into countless homes.

Just as the unadorned décor of the modernist movement was reflected a few decades later in the ultra-modern interiors of the jet age, so twenty-first century home-owners are rediscovering the elegance of mid-century furniture and using it to create timeless interiors. The beauty and aesthetic harmony of the designs, together with the high-quality materials and workmanship, have been rewarded with a renaissance in mid-century furniture that seems here to stay.

Designed by architects

By the time the mid-century dawned, furniture was no longer seen as an isolated craft but as part of a continuum of design. Architecture and each element within the interior design of a building were intertwined, with furniture considered to be the essence of the modern interior.

Although the impact of the new architectural style was immediate, the furniture industry lagged slightly behind. Furniture manufacturers commissioned designs from architects, who transformed the bespoke furniture they had made for their clients into designs that could be produced in multiples.

For many architects, furniture design was a satisfactory and rewarding art. Although a completed building could take years to construct, furniture could move from the drawing board to the showroom in a matter of months. Even so, architects continued to approach the design of furniture in the same way as for a building, basing their designs on enduring classical elements rather than fleeting aesthetic trends. Like architecture, furniture revolves around the proportions of the human body, and architects regarded tables and chairs as the link between the built environment and man's need for physical comfort.

Many of the celebrated designers of American mid-century furniture were actually European-born architects. Ludwig Mies van der Rohe, who was condemned by the Nazi regime for his high-minded aesthetics, moved to the United States from his native Germany in 1938, after the closure of the Bauhaus school of design, of which he had been the director. Mies, as his new home dubbed him, became head of the Department of Architecture at the Armour Institute in Chicago, where he had also established his own practice. While his American contemporaries were busy producing new furniture, Mies quietly reintroduced his designs from the 1920s and '30s. His chrome and leather Barcelona series was virtually the embodiment of mid-century modernism, despite having been designed in 1929. His maxim that 'less is more' completely redefined how architects saw their buildings, and revolutionized furniture design for ever.

Like Mies, Marcel Breuer also pioneered the modernist aesthetics of the Bauhaus in the United States. Born in Hungary in 1902, Breuer studied at the Academy of Art in Vienna before training at the Bauhaus. He worked as an architect in continental Europe and in England before being invited by Walter Gropius to teach at Harvard. Breuer's radical Wassily armchair in chrome-plated tubular steel was designed in 1925 and immediately became a gleaming icon of the modernist movement. His Laccio tables and his Cesca chair, all designed in 1928, were equally innovative. All were widely popular in Europe and North America during the 1950s, and they continue to be manufactured today.

Paul Laszlo left his native Hungary to study architecture in Vienna, Paris and Berlin before moving to Los Angeles in 1936. Whereas his European colleagues were known for the restraint and understatement they introduced, Laszlo's lavish style was pure Hollywood. He established himself through special commissions for stars such as Cary Grant, Elizabeth Taylor and Barbara Stanwyck, and clients who lived in the opulent mansions of Beverly Hills and Bel Air. Laszlo's heavy, overstuffed pieces were luxuriously upholstered in quilted silk and were denied any trace of an architectural signature, but their solid mass and sectional designs were superbly conceived and expertly crafted.

BELOW Arne Jacobsen created versatile shapes that could be adapted to a range of functions. His Series 7 chairs, from 1955, could be fitted with different bases: the 3217, shown here, had castors. The Home Office desk was designed by George Nelson in 1948.

[Mid-century craftsmen regarded furniture as an incomplete art, requiring a seated human to accomplish the aim of the design.]

TOP LEFT Charles and Ray Eames pioneered many of the twentieth century's most influential designs, including the FSW8 canvas and moulded-plywood eight-panel screen; the fibreglass, wood and zinc wire RAR chair; and the free-standing ESU 400-C cabinet (see page 89), all icons of mid-century style.

BOTTOM LEFT An Eames ETR (Surfboard) table of 1950 sits by a George Nelson Coconut chair of 1955 (see pages 104 and 105).

RIGHT The Eames 670 lounge chair and 671 ottoman, from 1958, were exquisitely crafted in rosewood and soft calfskin. The chair was divided into three sections joined by aluminium clips.

Born in Finland, Eero Saarinen emigrated to the United States with his parents, Eliel and Loja Saarinen. After his graduation from Yale, Eero pursued a career in architecture and design, also lecturing at Cranbrook Academy of Art as his father had. His big breakthrough as an architect came when he was commissioned to design the General Motors Technical Center. As a designer, his technique of making moulded fibreglass furniture revolutionized the industry, making him an international name. Pieces such as the Womb chair (1948), the Tulip chair (1956) and other pedestal-based furniture anticipated the organic contours and wavy structures of 1960s and '70s architecture.

Saarinen baffled his American contemporaries when he stated that the chair was a component of its architectural environment. He left them speechless by saying that the chair remained an unfinished design – only when a human meshed with the chair by sitting in it could it be considered complete.

Charles Eames studied architecture before accepting a fellowship at Cranbrook. Together with his wife, Ray Kaiser Eames, Charles Eames designed an influential steel-framed house made with standard prefabricated parts in 1949. Today, however, the couple are best remembered for their furniture.

Another American, Florence Knoll also studied at Cranbrook Academy of Art and then graduated from the Architectural Association in London. After training with Mies van der Rohe for a year, she began working for Walter Gropius in 1940. The painted steel rods, plywood backing and rectilinear foam shapes of her early chairs foreshadowed the juxtaposition of streamlined mass and transparency that mid-century architecture would later introduce. Knoll's works often integrated several individual pieces in one design, typically combining an upholstered couch and a wooden side table by joining them on a steel base. In 1955 Knoll became head of her family's firm, the furniture and interior design company Knoll Associates (now Knoll International).

LEFT The steel and glass of skyscrapers and residential architecture were mirrored in furniture constructed from the same materials. The polished chrome and glass of this mid-century table almost vanishes as it enables the set of Jacobsen dining chairs to be visible beneath its surface. In this interior the owner has deliberately chosen furniture that communicates with the interior architecture.

George Nelson was a furniture designer, an interior designer and a published writer, as well as an architect. He studied at Yale, going on to win the Prix de Rome for architecture in 1932. Nelson's interests and accomplishments were diverse; he is best known for weightless daybeds with breathtakingly thin frames, simplified desks and sculptural seating (see page 105). The brilliance of his square, cabinet-like steel-framed cases, miniature cabinets and modular systems (see page 90) was attributed to the architectural nature of their construction.

The Japanese-American designer George Nakashima studied architecture in the United States and then worked for Antonin Raymond's practice in Japan and India. Nakashima was interned during the war, but he set up his own furniture studio soon after being released. His work during the 1950s reflected Shaker influences, combined with elements of Windsor chair design and the elegance of the Japanese tradition. Nakashima liked the combination of raw, organic materials and sleek, polished surfaces. His acclaimed chaise longue in walnut with woven cloth suspension and his three-drawer sideboard in walnut and raffia exemplify this aspect of his style.

Arne Jacobsen was Denmark's most celebrated post-war architect. His early work was heavily influenced by modernists such as Le Corbusier, Gropius and Gunnar Asplund, and he was able to progress their ideas significantly in his own work. His vision for the Royal Hotel in Copenhagen was to interrelate the building's structure and its interior elements within a single design idiom. With the colleagues from his practice, he succeeded in designing the building and every single architectural detail within it, as well as all the furniture and interior accessories, plus the cutlery (flatware) and crockery, between 1955 and 1960.

Verner Panton worked alongside Jacobsen after training as an architect at the Royal Danish Academy of Fine Arts. Panton assisted Jacobsen with experimental furniture designs before establishing his own design studio in 1955.

Gio Ponti was born in Italy and educated in Milan, where he opened his own architectural studio in 1927 and then launched the architectural magazine *Domus* one year later. In 1932 Ponti founded Fontana Arte, which manufactured his lighting designs, and in the 1950s he became renowned for such classics as the angular Distex armchair (1954) and the elegant Superleggera chair (1957). Ponti's architectural projects overtook his furniture commissions towards the end of his life.

ABOVE Jacobsen's Egg chair (see page 100), designed in 1956, was an architectural environment in itself. Although the design is streamlined, the chairs rarely look right in small spaces, as they were intended to create a cosy enclave within a large room. The shape of the chair allows the seated person to nestle into a cocoon-like enclosure.

Modern classics

Furniture has today become a hallmark of mid-century style, and the passion to own original pieces from the 1950s has never been stronger. Mid-century furniture has defied the cult of the collectable to increase in value and appeal as the years go by. The unique balance of beauty, comfort, luxury and utility captured in mid-century pieces gives them timeless appeal, and their purity and simplicity make them seem contemporary today. While the designs are remarkable for the sheer virtuosity of their craftsmanship, the high quality of the materials used to produce them has enabled them to withstand the test of time. As minimalism resurfaced in the 1990s, classic designs from the 1950s were reintroduced to the contemporary interior, where their understated decorative features and sculptural silhouettes complemented recent designs.

During the 1950s, the structure of furniture became both lightweight and streamlined, with new construction techniques making it possible to craft visible frameworks that were pleasing to the eye. Designers such as Arne Jacobsen, Jean Prouvé and Finn Juhl pared down decorative features to a mere suggestion of ornamentation, then stripped away excess padding and upholstery to bring the underlying supports directly into view. This enabled the outer surfaces to become streamlined, as they no longer concealed a complicated inner structure. Such designs capture the spirit of mid-century furniture but still seem contemporary, largely because they remain unblemished by the motifs and ornamentation that 'date' furniture for ever.

Among the sleekest designs of the 1950s were the sideboards, credenzas (sideboards with shelves at the ends) and modular units made by Danish craftsmen. Denmark had excelled at cabinetmaking for several centuries, and its modern furniture designers drew upon this rich history.

A pioneer of 'floating' forms, Finn Juhl designed sideboards, shelving units and wooden cabinets with fixtures that anchored them to the wall so they were suspended over the floor. Juhl also designed many pieces anchored to a wooden base with legs that stood a foot or two above the floor, which allowed them to clear skirting boards (baseboards) and stand flush against the wall.

Finn Juhl's Chieftain chair, designed in 1949, has been reintroduced, but vintage originals are rarely seen outside museum collections. The Chieftain features a low-slung seat and tapering back, which peak into horn-like configurations in each corner. The armrests spill over the frame in undulating curves that recall organic shapes. Although he worked with a wide range of woods, teak was Juhl's material of choice, and his influence led to the widespread use of teak in modern Scandinavian furniture, contributing to the Danish 'teak style' of the 1950s.

Hans Wegner began his furniture career in the late 1920s, working as a cabinetmaker. He teamed up with fellow Danish designer Børge Mogensen in 1946. Like Juhl and Jacobsen, they were instrumental in launching the Danish Modern style, which showed the world that Denmark had more to export than just cabinets. Wegner's wood and leather armchairs were as highly prized then as now, as were his low teak and aluminium side tables. His Papa Bear chair (1954), an overstuffed wing chair, was crafted with both arms outstretched as if its 'paws' were ready to embrace its occupant.

The African influence that swept Scandinavia also inspired furniture designs in Britain. Ernest Race's Antelope chair, with its spindly legs terminating in ball feet, debuted at the Festival of Britain in 1951. It had an enamelled steel-rod frame and a simple moulded-plywood seat. His Springbok chair was stackable, with elastic cords

ABOVE Mid-century dining suites were superbly crafted in a variety of beautiful woods ranging from wenge and teak to oak, maple and cherry. This elegant sideboard features a double cabinet for china and tableware, with four drawers for storing cutlery (flatware) and table linen. The drop-leaf table seats four for a cosy dinner or extends to accommodate eight dinner guests.

stretched around its steel-rod frame and crafted into a seat and backrest. He also designed furniture using a material called Holoplast, a plastic laminate with a highly polished, scratch-resistant mahogany-coloured finish resembling wood. Race concealed the joins of the table surface with a thin ribbon of aluminium, which was heat-shrunk to cap the edges. His wooden furniture rose from the floor on tapering legs, generating a weightless effect that contrasted with the heavy, low-slung furniture produced by many of his British contemporaries. Race was known for advancing the contemporary look in Britain, and his original pieces strongly evoke the spirit of the era.

In Italy Marco Zanuso and Franco Albini interpreted the new furniture movement as an expression of luxury and style. The armchair, in their eyes, was a mini comfort zone, padded and elasticated to promote relaxation, and sculpted in fluid abstractions to express a sense of movement. Zanuso's Lady armchair (1951) was made from four mass-produced foam components upholstered and assembled to look like a custom-made chair. He designed another armchair in 1954, the Martingala, which featured in many Italian homes of the period. Albini's Fiorenza armchair (1952) was divided into two units: a high-rising backrest incorporating the arms, and a low-slung, angle-poised seat.

The separate parts were interconnected by a wooden X-shape on either side. Fiorenza, like Zanuso's Lady, was considered esoteric, and vintage models are difficult to locate today.

The Dutch designer Friso Kramer played a significant role in the development of the modernist aesthetic in The Netherlands. Kramer was part of the Goed Wonen ('Good Living') movement of the 1950s. It was committed to creating a new national style despite the economic hardship and scarcity of materials that followed the war. One of Kramer's contributions was the Revolt chair (1953), which featured a moulded-plywood seat that curved gently at the front edge, joined to a separate cupped backrest by a steel frame. Revolt was a standard fixture in households and schools for several decades and is considered a classic today.

From 1955, and continuing well into the 1960s, another Dutch designer, Cees Braakman, who was also a part of the Goed Wonen movement, devoted much of his attention to the design of modular cabinets, creating a flexible system that provided homemakers with a range of woods and interchangeable components to choose from. It is a system that still works today, and Braakman's vintage teak and white Formica wall units are highly prized by Dutch collectors.

While many of the furniture designs by Charles and Ray Eames are in production today, iconic chairs such as the Cat's Cradle fibreglass chair (1952), the RAR rocking armchair (1951 – pictured on page 82) and the PKW wire swivel chair (1951) are among the most popular vintage pieces. The durable construction of the steel wire frames that these four pieces rest on often remains in pristine condition, and the fibreglass shells of the chairs are resistant to colour fading and water damage, holding their shapes despite decades of use. The collection of chairs in the series that is known as 'Aluminum, Fiberglass and Vinyl' superimposes a curving, vinyl-covered fibreglass form atop a four-pointed aluminium stand with rounded 'feet'. Models from this series come up regularly at auction and on Internet websites.

Pieces such as their free-standing ESU 400-C cabinet (pictured on page 82), in aluminium, Masonite and plywood held together by a steel frame, reflected their architectural ethos. In

ABOVE LEFT Pivoting segments combine the compartmentalized spaces of a cabinet with the sliding accessibility of a chest of drawers.

LEFT In the 1950s, daybeds and divans replaced overstuffed sprung sofas. This Danish daybed, called a 'bumper' settee because of the adjustable armrest, was designed with a removable sprung seat and backrest, and a detachable armrest that could be fitted at either end. A Model 75 chair by Niels Ole Møller (1956) is on the right.

ABOVE A pair of Marco Zanuso's Lady armchairs attest to the deceptive comfort of 1950s classics.

ABOVE New styles of furniture took centre stage in the 1950s, bearing the distinctive shapes that announce the mid-century look today. The 'bubbled' veneer of the Eames sliding-door ESU cabinet, made of plywood, Masonite and aluminium, introduced a novel texture to wood furniture.

ABOVE RIGHT George Nelson's Marshmallow sofa (see page 105) relied on a simple geometric repeat and a skeletal metal frame to supply one of the decade's most acclaimed furniture innovations. In front is Isamu Noguchi's wood and glass coffee table and an Eames fibreglass DAR chair.

1956 they began developing the series later known as the Aluminum Group of high-back lounge chairs for a private residence being designed by Eero Saarinen and Alexander Girard. Each chair's steel construction, tilt–swivel mechanism and comfortable suspension constituted a feat of engineering, dramatically suspending the seated person over the base, so that they were cantilevered backwards.

Vintage pieces designed by George Nelson are slightly harder to come by than those by Charles and Ray Eames, despite their having been mass-produced for the North American market. Many of Nelson's works were recognized as design classics soon after they appeared, with pieces such as the Marshmallow sofa, Coconut chair, Sling sofa and Kangaroo chair acquired by the Museum of Modern Art in New York as early as 1964. Nelson's Comprehensive Storage System in aluminium and wood (1958) has provided a template for many other wall units, but few surpass the unassuming elegance and perfect proportions of his original design.

[The sculptural, sensual contours that characterize mid-century classics captured the modernist spirit, charging it with the vibrancy and optimism of youth culture.]

LEFT A balancing act of mass versus space, Arne Jacobsen's iconic Swan chair (see page 100), designed in 1958, possesses a throne-like gravitas despite having been designed as a humble low side chair. Jacobsen reduced the chair's bulk by combining the back, seat and arms in a single, graciously sculpted shell. Made from foam-upholstered moulded fibreglass, the seat was balanced atop a gleaming cast-aluminium swivelling pedestal base.

Organic style

Boomerangs, parabolas, ellipses and rhomboids – the so-called biomorphic shapes found in 1950s silhouettes – introduced a new formal language to furniture design, creating the free-flowing configurations known as kidney shapes, egg shapes, lozenges and cones. These spontaneous new forms displayed a balance between art and nature that referenced modern painting, abstract sculpture and wave-form architecture, while exploring biological discoveries and microscope views of molecules.

Biomorphic shapes were most popular in North America and Scandinavia, where they became known as organic designs. They were inspired by natural forms as well as nature itself. Swollen shapes and gestation forms characterized the work of some designers, who are said to have been inspired by the pregnant bellies of the post-war baby boom. Saarinen's Womb chair, Jacobsen's Egg chair, Nelson's Kangaroo and Coconut

BELOW The La Chaise lounge chair was designed in 1948 for a Museum of Modern Art competition by Charles and Ray Eames, who based its organic shape on the Floating Figure sculpture by Gaston Lachaise. Ahead of its time, it was not manufactured until 1991.

RIGHT This sideboard was designed by Booth & Ledeboer in mahogany and rosewood, with doors incised to reveal the light wood beneath the veneer.

BELOW RIGHT The incised decorations on this teak cupboard hint that it was designed as a dining sideboard.

chairs reference birth and renewal, while Wegner's Ox chair, Race's Antelope, Rebok and Flamingo chairs, and Saarinen's Grasshopper chair and Tulip series explore living forms in nature.

Organic forms were the antithesis of the machine aesthetic introduced by the earlier modernist movement, and counteracted the geometric modernism espoused by Mies van der Rohe in the United States. Although aesthetics changed dramatically, modernist materials prevailed, with glass, metal and concrete used to create organic forms rather than geometric ones.

New plywood technology allowed multi-directional curves, and developments in mouldable fibreglass and synthetic foams meant that these shapes could be contoured and comfortable. Such innovations enabled the new generation of designers to interpret furniture as sculptural form, treating functionality as a basis for aesthetic expression. Studies in the role of form and the relationships between materials were initiated, and elements such as air and negative space were acknowledged as part of the design idiom, just as transparency was playing a prominent role in interior architecture.

As early as 1940, Eero Saarinen had collaborated with Charles Eames to develop a body-moulded plywood chair that combined the seat, backrest and arms in a single consolidated shell form. The result was a landmark design, mirroring the profile of the seated body but also revealing the beauty of curvilinear shapes. By engineering their organic designs for mass production, they set a precedent for 1950s furniture. Saarinen's curvilinear outlines were echoed in the swelling roofs and wavy concrete walls of his building blueprints, creating a lively dialogue between furniture and architecture.

In the United States, Vladimir Kagan was considered a pioneer of organic design. During a career that spanned more than fifty years, his amorphous, sculptural shapes of the late 1940s and early '50s created a new look in American furniture. His kidney-shaped travertine coffee table (1952) was designed with three sculpted walnut legs to support the sensuous contours of its travertine surface. In 1958, Kagan designed a 'floating seat and back curved sofa', which had a sweeping crescent-shaped

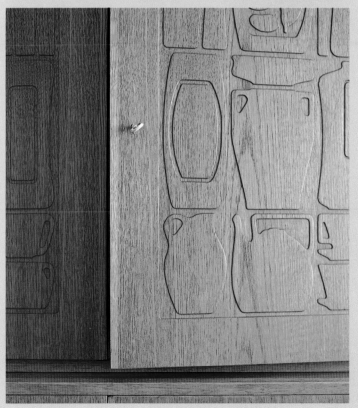

seat mirrored by a contoured backrest placed above it. Three sculpted walnut legs were fitted at intervals along the seat, each arcing upwards to form a support for the sofa's back. Today Kagan's original organic designs are coveted by collectors for their original features and enduring craftsmanship. The demand has led to the introduction of his new wavy Dot.com sofa, a biomorphic design made with adjustable cushion seats at varied heights that can be reconfigured into several different shapes.

In Isamu Noguchi's hands abstract art became applied art. In one of his sculptures, wood and glass were moulded into an arrestingly curvaceous silhouette that caught the eye of George Nelson, who identified the shape of a table in its form. An American manufacturer shared Nelson's view and in 1944 collaborated with Noguchi to transform the design into a coffee table. Organic in style, Noguchi's Coffee Table was manufactured with two wooden legs that interlocked to form a tripod, which supported a plate-glass top 2cm (¾in) thick. Both parts of the design were reversible: the tabletop could be placed upside down or back to front, while the mirror effect of the tripod's design enabled it to maintain the same profile even when turned upside down. Needless to say, Noguchi's considered balance of sculptural form, design innovation and durable function inspired other designers of the period to pursue abstract shapes.

By the time the 1950s dawned, Pierre Paulin had been designing furniture for more than two decades. His early work featured the curvaceous silhouettes of the art nouveau and art deco styles, and vestiges of the classical shapes from those traditions can be identified in the organic designs that he produced three decades later. Paulin's Orange Slice chair (1957) was constructed from two crescent-like upholstered segments joined to a four-legged metal base. The segments united at the point where the seat and backrest met and then curved outwards to create a sloping, conical form.

[Cloud shapes, amoeba-like forms, undulating lines and resounding curves are hallmarks of biomorphic design.]

LEFT From 1957 to 1972, Erwine and Estelle Laverne designed a series of transparent chairs, known as the Invisible Group, which were intended to create a greater sense of space in their setting. These early examples were produced in malleable Lucite plastic that is easily moulded into organic shapes.

In Italy designs by Carlo Mollino revealed a subtle link between the radical shapes of organic style and the dynamic forms of the Futurist movement. Mollino's Arabesque table (1950) balanced a plate of curving glass atop an S-shaped base that supported the glass near each end. The sharp curves of the base captured movement between them, which Mollino juxtaposed with the tranquillity of the smooth glass to create a study of stillness and motion. Likewise, the exaggerated, robust contours of the armchair Mollino designed with Aldo Morbelli for the RAI auditorium in Turin combined sensuous, rounded shapes with the repeated movements of a machine aesthetic, which they captured in an organic profile.

One of Italy's signature biomorphic designs was Valberto Zeller's ACMA coffee table (1950). It featured a stoneware slab tabletop which was abstractly contoured into a heart-like profile and embellished with wavy lines that emanated from a tight spiral in the centre, spreading wider apart as they reached the edges of the table surface. ACMA was one of the first Italian designs to merge a biomorphic motif with an organic shape.

Erwine and Estelle Laverne were pioneers of moulded furniture who promoted a range of organic and biomorphic designs. Trading under the name Laverne International, the couple marketed their own designs as well as collaborations with artists such as Alexander Calder and architects such as Oscar Niemeyer. While their acclaimed New Furniture Group mirrored the curvilinear shapes introduced by other designers of organic furniture, their Invisible Group of moulded Lucite furniture showcased something completely new. From 1957 the Lavernes' transparent plastic furniture included orb-like chairs that appeared to cocoon those seated in plastic bubbles. The chair's back, seat and arms were smoothed into a single contour, attached to a sloping pedestal of clear plastic.

The dense surface of Willy Guhl's Loop chair (1954) was the antithesis of the Lavernes' translucent designs. Loop was constructed from a single ribbon of Eternit, a cement and fibre-bond material, which sloped sharply downwards from the back before abruptly bending into the seat and continuing back to its starting point. The design was rather abstract, but the effect created a distinguishable chair silhouette with a hollow interior. Remembering the chair's success, Guhl introduced a low Loop table in 1999, designed to nest inside the chair. As Guhl revisits the biomorphic shape in his furniture today, organic style seems set for a twenty-first century revival.

ABOVE The Harp, or String, chair was designed by Jorgen Hovelskov in 1957. While the cherry frame and taut strings recall a musical instrument, the curved shapes of the structure were actually inspired by the prows of Viking ships.

ABOVE Many pieces designed by Alvar Aalto, Charles and Ray Eames and Hans Wegner look completely at ease in modern homes. Aalto's beech Y 601 stool and Model 84 table have been in continuous production since the 1950s. The padded wire seat of the Eames DKR-2 chair was inspired by wire baskets and metal cages. The chair is no longer in production.

RIGHT Wegner's Model 501 armchair is crafted in teak with a woven rattan seat and backrest. The chair has never seemed outdated since its debut in 1949.

FAR RIGHT Jean Prouvé's Antony chair was designed in 1954 and reintroduced in the twenty-first century. The chair's industrial frame blurs the boundaries between contract furniture and the avant-garde.

Contemporary icons

The furniture of the forward-thinking 1950s designers has never dated, and many designs have been produced continuously since they were introduced more than half a century ago. The designers of the mid-twentieth century merged natural elements, expressive materials and vibrant colours into stylish and streamlined pieces that revived the concepts of functionality and stylistic harmony introduced by the modernists many years earlier. These principles continue to underpin the homes of the twenty-first century, and the demand for the iconic furniture of the 1950s has never been stronger.

As the craze for 1950s furniture takes hold, the past is being given an inspiring new twist by the present, signalling a fresh direction for the hallmarks of the mid-century era. Today's chic interiors feature new editions of classic designs, manufactured to look as crisp and novel as they did half a century ago. While the demand for famous favourites continues to grow, many manufacturers have also reintroduced lesser-known designs that are even more popular today than during the 1950s.

Such is the case with Jean Prouvé's work, which is receiving considerable international attention today. His furniture was hardly known outside of his native France, but now designs like the EM table and the Prouvé Standard chair feature in homes all over the world. The streamlined Antony chair, developed in 1954, has a wood-veneer seat atop a svelte steel frame that cradles its dynamic sweep and is supported by a four-legged base crafted from two steel rods bent into a V-shape.

Two of Prouvé's tables have also been reintroduced. The Trapèze table (1950–54) has a heavy laminate tabletop poised across two black-lacquered steel bases resting on four feet, and takes its name from its unique balancing act. The elegant EM table (1950) is also designed with a slanting base made of sheet metal, with each tapered leg turning out and angling diagonally to distribute the weight of the tabletop from its centre down to the floor. The tabletop is crafted in wood veneer, lending a warm counterpoint to the mechanical efficiency of the metal base.

[The enduring appeal of mid-century furniture is attributed to the creation of beautiful designs that offered practical solutions for everyday living.]

Hans Wegner's flawless furniture has never dated, and he is now considered one of Denmark's greatest furniture designers. The sophisticated lines of Wegner's chairs cleverly balance formal characteristics against functionalist ease. Many of his designs echo the elegance of China's Ming Dynasty in the manner in which the armrests and back merge gracefully into one another. His Round chair of 1949 was based on such time-honoured principles, but he also introduced a number of forward-thinking innovations, such as the three-legged Valet chair, designed to be a smart extension of a clothes cupboard. The backrest was crafted in the shape of a coat hanger, and the flattened seat given contoured edges for trousers and neckties to be laid across. The Flag Halyard (1950) takes its name from the flag halyard cord wound around the chromed tubular steel pipes of its frame and woven into a seat covered with fleece. Unlike the Round and Valet chairs, the Flag Halyard is unique in that it has no historical precedent. Likewise, the Ox chair (1959–60), a low-slung, overstuffed easy chair, took Wegner's work in a new direction. It was designed with wings pitched sideways like a pair of horns, superbly bridging the gap between elegance and playfulness.

Arne Jacobsen's iconic Swan chair (pictured on page 91) also moves between playful innovation and classical sophistication but was developed with the emphasis on comfort rather than multi-functionality. Like the accompanying two-seater Swan sofa, it was designed in 1958 for the Royal Hotel in Copenhagen. Other enduring pieces have remained in production more or less continuously since they were first produced. Jacobsen's Ant chair, which virtually became his signature design, was crafted from a single piece of laminated wood curved into a seat and backrest divided by a 'waist'. This shell rested on a minimalist base of three interconnected legs crafted from burnished chrome-plated steel tubing. Only after Jacobsen's death was the chair painted, as he never allowed the design to be adulterated by paint or surface motifs during his lifetime.

The Ant chair was followed in 1955 by the Series 7 chairs (one of which is pictured on page 81) and the Tongue chair, also designed with an emphasis on weightlessness and sculptural simplicity. Jacobsen crafted legs and pedestal bases as thin as possible, coating them in chrome so their substance would dissolve in reflections. To him such slender pedestals created a simplicity not found in a mass of angled lines. This design device gave all of his chairs a 'floating' effect that counteracted their weight and density.

Jacobsen designed his iconic Egg lounge chair in 1956 in his garage, where he cast the entire shell in plaster as though creating a curvaceous sculpture. Once the shape was perfected, the shell was produced in lighter materials, then padded with cold foam and covered with fabric or leather. The seat, back and armrests were created in a single expression that curved upwards over and around the occupant, creating the feeling of sitting within a protective enclosure. Conceiving a chair that could generate a sense

THIS PAGE Almost every one of Arne Jacobsen's designs is regarded as a contemporary icon. The Model 3107 dining chairs, shown here, were designed in 1955. Each has a one-piece moulded-plywood seat and backrest to which different bases, arms and veneers could be attached. The 3107s remain among the most commercially successful designs every produced.

of seclusion was genius on Jacobsen's part, as it reinstated the solitude sacrificed to the open-plan layout of a room. When placed opposite each other, two Egg chairs create a feeling of privacy within a large space, and grouping three or four together builds a nest.

Few of Poul Kjærholm's designs have ever dated, which is probably why he continues to be a legend among Danish designers. He was some twenty years younger than Jacobsen, and his work exemplified a second wave of Danish design that found expression in strips of dynamic steel and metallic grids rather than bent plywood. He often combined a steel frame with fabric upholstery, leather or canework, as in his understated PK22 lounge chair (1955). His work moved in a new direction when his PK31, PK32 and PK33 sofas and easy chairs were introduced in 1958, as he juxtaposed dense, cubic, 'futuristic' shapes in supple black leather with curvaceous chromed metal bases. The sectional PK 31 sofa rested on a base of matt chromium-plated sprung steel. The units were produced in two- or three-seater sections, or in one section as an easy chair. His PK 80 (1957) daybed is an icon of contemporary cool, revealing parallels with the modernism of Mies van der Rohe and Le Corbusier. The couch was designed with a satin-brushed stainless-steel suspension frame and it has a sheath of painted plywood beneath its leather cushions. The succinct, and somewhat austere, design of Kjærholm's PK 61 coffee table (1955) is captivating in its geometric simplicity. The PK 61 clasps a sheet of dense glass within a steel frame through which its staggered legs are visible. It is clearly a table with nothing to hide, and reveals the beauty and harmony that result when the balance of sculptural form and everyday function is achieved.

Jens Risom, a Danish-American designer, designed one of North America's first lines of modern furniture in 1941. The furniture attracted limited interest during the war, but by the 1950s Risom's tables were found in modern homes throughout the United States. While many of his contemporaries were experimenting with metals and plastics, Risom preferred wood. His simple dining tables and side tables were designed with mortise-and-tenon joints to flat-pack for self-assembly. Their clean lines provided understated pieces that would easily coordinate with other furniture designs. Risom's curvaceous Amoeba coffee table anticipated the craze for biomorphic shapes that would mark the 1950s and, to his chagrin, was often imitated during his lifetime.

Eero Saarinen, like Risom, began developing a new design idiom in the 1940s that led to a breakthrough in 1948 with his celebrated Womb chair (pictured on page 80). Saarinen padded and upholstered the chair's fibreglass frame, setting it atop a chromed steel-rod base. The sensuous contours and sloping curves of the Womb chair had great impact, contributing to the demand for organic furniture that prevailed in the 1950s.

Saarinen's range of Tulip chairs, launched in 1956, eliminated the need for four legs by fitting the seat to the top of a rounded pedestal, which widened as it arced outwards at each end to support the seat. The Tulip simplified the traditional chair design by dividing it into two elements: a streamlined pedestal base and a shell-like moulded-fibreglass body that merged the seat, backrest and arms into a single component. The Tulip chair epitomized Saarinen's rallying cry for clean lines and led him to design a table based on the same principles. The Saarinen table (sometimes incorrectly referred to as a Tulip table), also launched in 1956, had a white laminate top with a bevel edge atop a cast-aluminium base coated with an abrasion-resistant white finish. The tables were initially designed as dining tables that could seat six, then as smaller versions. Particularly compatible with Tulip chairs, they marry well with virtually any modern chair.

BELOW Poul Kjærholm's PK22 chair was designed in 1955, its minimalistic silhouette recalling the simplified shape of Mies van der Rohe's Barcelona chair. Many of Kjærholm's designs were true to the modernist spirit, and Kjærholm was unusual among his Danish contemporaries in adopting steel rather than teak as his material of choice.

ABOVE These 1948 dining chairs by Eero Saarinen were part of his 72 Series of office chairs. Also available with metal legs and a wooden backrest, the chair was promoted by the manufacturer as a shining example of a contemporary office chair. The version shown here is constructed with a foam-lined shell upholstered in chenille fabric.

Many of the designs by Charles and Ray Eames have 'retro appeal', but connoisseurs would argue that their furniture has never gone out of style. A remarkable high number of their designs are still in production today: their Moulded Plywood Folding Screen (1946), black leather and wood-veneer Lounge Chair with Ottoman (1956), boldly original Eames Desk Unit (1952) and Storage Unit (1950), and streamlined, mechanized Aluminum Group chairs (1956) are striking examples of how these leaders in experimentation extended the boundaries of design.

Their influential designs often combined surprising shapes with unconventional materials. For their elliptical ETR, or 'Surfboard', table (pictured on page 82), designed in 1950, they opted for a low, lateral silhouette that stands comfortably in front of a long sofa and offers a dramatic display surface. The plywood and steel LTR was introduced in the following year, a 10in-high table designed as an ideal surface upon which to prepare the traditional Japanese tea ceremony. Recently reintroduced, these pieces are also practical for everyday use as unique display surfaces, bedside tables or plant stands.

When Charles and Ray Eames produced their first plastic chairs in 1950, they advanced the use of fibreglass-reinforced plastic for seating. Their single-shell plastic models rested on a bent-wire welded support known as the 'Eiffel Tower' base, as they do today. When they were first designed, their impact was immediate; because they were lightweight, sturdy and easy to move, they became a favourite choice for offices as well as the home. Although the current models look exactly the same as the originals, they have been updated with an environmentally friendly, durable plastic shell.

The American sculptor Harry Bertoia adapted the bent metal rods used in his artwork for the functional art of sculptural furniture. He had collaborated with Charles and Ray Eames, who had been among the first designers to pioneer the use of bent and welded wire as the basis for furniture. Bertoia's small Diamond lounge chair (c.1952) is considered one of the best mid-century designs in production today. Originally crafted from welded steel rods with a black or white nylon-dipped finish,

it was designed with a seat cushion in red or black vinyl secured by snaps to the seat. Today the chair frame is produced in a finish of polished satin chrome, with full-cover upholstery or cushions in a variety of fabrics or leather.

Many of George Nelson's iconic designs reflect his architectural training. With its plain, rectilinear lines and simple wooden construction, Nelson's Platform Bench (1946) makes an immediate statement about its function and materials. Reintroduced in 1994, the Platform Bench is a resting place for both people and objects, and its striking design has looked contemporary for more than five decades. His Coconut chair (pictured on page 82), which was introduced in 1955, is also a mid-century classic. The chair was designed as a moulded-plastic shell fitted to a three-legged chromed-steel base, thickly padded with foam rubber and upholstered in leather or fabric. With its shallow sides and inviting curves, the chair facilitates a range of comfortable sitting positions that allow the occupant to relax completely.

Nelson's Marshmallow sofa (pictured on page 90) is a landmark of modern design and a collectable icon today. When it was introduced in 1956, the manufacturer regarded it as a new concept in soft seating as well as a vision of future furniture aesthetics. Nelson designed a linear metal frame which he concealed with eighteen round cushions. The Marshmallow could be purchased either with all the cushions in the same fabric, or individually upholstered in a multitude of colours. Reintroduced in 1999, it is in such high demand today that it appears to have a cult following.

ABOVE LEFT Harry Bertoia's Diamond chairs, designed in 1952, are highly versatile. Their lightweight structure and see-through design suit a wide range of dining furniture.

ABOVE A pedestal table is surrounded by chrome and rosewood DCM chairs designed by Charles and Ray Eames in 1958. The DCM's metal structure and thin wooden parts were meant to dissolve as much of its mass as possible, enabling it to coordinate with a wide range of furnishings.

DESIGN DETAILS

The quest for the perfect form was an obsession that guided many mid-century designers, provoking a dramatic break with conventional shapes and time-honoured techniques.

While functional objects have always been regarded as the tools of the home, their potential to express artistic sentiments was widely recognized in the 1950s, and many designs were created with a sculptural dimension that transcended their utility. The consumer boom that began in the 1950s led to increased mass production, but as glass, metal, ceramics and wood were manipulated in factories, they lost the sense of unique expression that hand-crafting gave them. For many homemakers the machine aesthetic of mechanical production epitomized progress and innovation, but for others the absence of the human touch signified a decline in craftsmanship.

With this in mind, many designers coupled streamlined efficiency with a sense of artistic élan, or found methods of making prefabricated goods that would still appear unique to the homemaker. Natural materials such as cane or rattan were added to mimic a handicraft element, while hand-turned wooden handles enabled a streamlined tea set to convey comfort and warmth. As they incorporated craft elements, mid-century designs were symbolically aligned to traditional skills and craft techniques, anchoring modern objects to the splendours of the past.

Large-scale factory kilns began to emulate the hand-thrown 'studio' look in their pottery multiples, and glass manufacturers used labels to promote hand-blown pieces and differentiate them from pressed glass. Traditional glass craftsmen and old-school potters were replaced by artists and ceramicists, many of whom had studied their craft in colleges and universities and were motivated by a belief in the purity of form and the importance of design excellence. The role of ceramics and glass in the home took on new layers of meaning as pottery and glassware became more design-conscious, with products created to reflect studies in ergonomics or kinetic movement, or enhance the taste of wine and take into account the effects of temperature.

Although mid-century pieces are characterized by biomorphic forms and free-form shapes, many designers of the 1950s embarked on a quest for accuracy and precision. The influential Danish Modern furniture style was founded on principles of efficiency as well as functionalism, and this also sparked a drive to find ideal proportions for all household utensils. Cutlery (flatware) sizes became roughly standardized in length as designers arrived at the perfect proportions for drawers in a dining sideboard, and sets of china became stackable in order to be stored more easily. Tumblers were also produced in stacking designs and sets of bowls were made to nest easily, while utility ranges of dinnerware featured oven-to-table cookware coupled with lids that doubled as serving platters.

The beauty and efficiency of household items from all the Nordic countries in particular influenced the output of many designers around the world. The inspirational Design in Scandinavia exhibition was inaugurated in 1954, and then continued on a three-and-a half-year tour of the United States and Canada. In addition to showcasing streamlined furniture, the exhibition presented crystal and glassware from Sweden, enamelled metalware from Norway and Denmark, and ceramics, drinking glasses and cutlery from Finland. The exhibition promoted a new way of living with functional objects, emphasizing the properties of good design and the beauty of natural materials. None of the Design in Scandinavia exhibits was given luxury status, in accordance with the concept of democratic design that had formed the basis of Nordic products for several decades.

Living with contemporary style was something of an obsession for American homemakers, who regularly attended exhibitions of modern living held in department stores, at trade fairs and in show homes. They learned how to 'mix and match' different dinner sets according to their styles and colours, and lay the table with ceramic centrepieces and metalware candelabra. From the more practical angle, housewives were shown that food could be stylishly served, prepared and stored in a single unbreakable, antibacterial, Tupperware plastic container.

Americans introduced a vogue for informal entertaining at home that spread to other nations as the decade wore on. Chic glassware for serving mixed drinks and sleek stemware for drinking wine were essential ingredients for the contemporary homemaker, who also arranged canapés on side plates, glass flats, or sectional 'hostess plates'. With the fashion for cocktails came the etiquette of mixing them in a range of different glasses, which could be purchased in sets complete with a serving tray and an ice bucket. Smoking became an art form, with sets of ashtrays, table lighters and cigarette boxes designed in matching enamelware or fine porcelain.

Far from being diminished, the appeal of mid-century glassware, ceramics, china and metalware has been enhanced by the passage of time, and many pieces are now highly collectable. Mid-century motifs and geometric patterns can inject today's interior with bright drama or colourful kitsch, while the sculptural charm of glass and ceramics adds a note of flamboyance and flair. Streamlined metalware and simple wooden pieces not only have an irresistible appeal to minimalists but will also provide the interior with ageless classics that may even outlast their owners.

Ceramics

The mid-century decade ushered in a new era for ceramics, marrying craft skills to modern design practice as aesthetic features were balanced against functionality. From the rough, intricate textures thrown on a potter's wheel to the refined shapes inspired by the ceramics of the Far East, the infinite possibilities of clay were explored to the full. The ceramics of the 1950s, whether crafted in streamlined, functional pieces that were manufactured industrially, or expressed in conceptual sculptures produced in studio workshops, revealed the artistic potential of clay. As ceramics gained an elevated status, potters were upgraded from artisans to artists, and the field was recognized as a fine art rather than a craft.

The biomorphic silhouettes and the asymmetrical shapes expressed in furniture and glass of the time had a huge impact on ceramics, influencing the work of ceramicists throughout Europe and North America. The simple shapes and banded decorations that had characterized Scandinavian ceramics for several decades morphed into undulating contours, rippling surfaces and irregular silhouettes.

Wilhelm Kåge, who for several decades had been regarded as one of Sweden's leading ceramicists, shook off his shrewd sense of design economy and created pieces with sculptural silhouettes, even conceiving hybrid forms and organic shapes that appeared to fuse art and nature. The voluptuous contours of Våga, Kåge's range of white stoneware vessels, appeared to melt into delicately fluted rims, while his moulded Terra Spirea stoneware resembled pod-like organic forms.

Stig Lindberg had trained under Kåge before taking over from him as the artistic director of the Gustavsberg kilns in 1949. Lindberg's approach to ceramics was organic, expressing itself in simple lines and bold contours. Throughout the 1950s his designs were acknowledged as prime examples of Scandinavian modernism. Lindberg's elliptical forms had an organic elegance that was new to Nordic ceramics. Virtually devoid of integral ornamentation, his strong, bold designs were produced in asymmetrical shapes and were decorated with striking, often whimsical motifs inspired by Scandinavian folk symbols. The

LEFT Many of the ceramic pieces featured here belong to American Modern, a multicoloured set of dinnerware designed by Russel Wright. First produced in 1939, it was indisputably the most popular china used in American homes during the 1950s – more than 80 million pieces had been sold by the end of the decade. Celebrated for its biomorphic shapes and its simple, organic lines streamlined into rimless forms, American Modern is a favourite of many mid-century collectors today.

[Ceramics grew more refined during the 1950s as craftsmen balanced their esoteric and aesthetic features against their functional use.]

ABOVE The Swedish ceramicist Stig Lindberg was one of the world's leading ceramicists during the 1950s, with an unchallenged repertoire of fluid, sculptural shapes and understated functional pieces. This classic stoneware vase, which was designed for Gustavsberg, is reminiscent of the simple faïence pieces he created during the 1940s.

arresting Pouch vase of 1953 was moulded into an elongated teardrop shape, with an extended asymmetrical mouth that dipped into a deep opening along the face of the vase.

Gunnar Nylund moved easily between the Swedish and Danish design traditions, producing prolifically in each. He had trained as an architect before beginning his career as a ceramic designer in Denmark at Bing & Grøndahl. He then co-founded the Saxbo stoneware studio with Nathalie Krebs in 1929. In 1931, Nylund returned to Sweden to act as Rörstrand's artistic director, but under Krebs's guidance Saxbo gained international acclaim. Saxbo pieces were widely exhibited throughout the 1950s and won a gold medal in 1957 at the Milan Triennale.

While Krebs created Saxbo's oriental-influenced glazes, her colleague Eva Staehr-Nielsen designed the simple, expertly crafted shapes that made the classic Saxbo style. In the late 1950s, Staehr-Nielsen moved from wheel-turned pottery to sculptural abstractions, often using incised patterns. Saxbo's heir apparent, if not its successor, was the Danish Palshus studio established by Per and Annelise Linnemann-Schmidt in 1948. The couple designed refined ceramics with simple glazes, producing beautiful, minimalist pieces partially inspired by Japanese raku potters. Per Linnemann-Schmidt was noted for his vases, bowls, figurines and teapots, and designed his own version of the spindle vase and triangular bowl, which are the most highly prized examples of his work today.

Across the Baltic the Finnish designer Kaj Franck began directing Arabia's design studio in 1945, introducing the revolutionary Kilta range of heat-resistant earthenware in 1948 and the highly collectable Snowball series in 1954. Towards the end of the decade, his colleague Ulla Procopé designed the innovative Flame range, in which the lids doubled as serving dishes. Procopé introduced a hand-crafted quality to Arabia's mass-produced designs by applying a mottled brown glaze, to resemble hand-thrown ceramics.

The work of Birger Kaipiainen, one of Finland's best-known ceramicists, is highly prized among collectors today. Kaipiainen devised designs almost exclusively for small-scale studio production, gaining recognition for his lavish colour-saturated motifs inspired by the extravagant ornamentation of the Byzantine and Renaissance styles.

During the 1950s and '60s Kaipiainen harvested nature's bounty for a crop of ripe fruits, decorating his ceramics in blossoming flowers and succulent berries which were so sensuous that they almost had erotic overtones.

The sensuality that characterized Kaipiainen's motifs was also found in the work of Italian ceramicists. The Florentine designer Marcello Fantoni gained acclaim for his luscious motifs and lustrous glazes, producing many large-scale vases and ewers with heavily textured surfaces. During the 1950s he was commissioned to design monumental figurative works and sculptural abstractions, and many of his pieces were based on container forms or inspired by Etruscan artefacts. Fantoni's handling of ancient influences was thoroughly modern, and his motifs, glazes and colour palettes continue to look contemporary today. His crisp silhouettes were coloured with boldly original combinations of rich earth tones and 'muddy' pastels that have never dated.

Also in Florence, Guido Gambone crafted exaggerated, expressive earthenware vessels coloured in vibrant hues for his Faenzerella ranges. His shapes were modern with a subtle suggestion of Etruscan pottery or early Greek ceramics, and his long-stemmed vases, squared platters and oblong vessels were decorated with simple line drawings, cubist-inspired patterns and abstract figures. He typically worked in reds, yellows and greens, which he deployed against a white or charcoal-grey background. Many of his abstract pieces were characterized by a wrapping technique that looked as if the clay had been folded into overlapping surfaces.

Antonia Campi was distinguished by her biomorphic shapes and sculptural silhouettes, and her work proved that ceramics could be an art form. The bulbous shapes and flowing stems of her vases expressed movement and fluidity, enhanced by sharply contrasting colourways glazed with a glossy sheen. Some of Campi's works suggested stylistic influences from the rococo period, while others recalled the legacy of the Italian Futurists or the work of surrealist artists such as Yves Tanguy.

Probably the most prolific Italian designer of the mid-century period, Piero Fornasetti produced a breathtaking array of ceramics. His pieces ranged from fine china and small boxes to ashtrays and desk sets, crafted in simple shapes that were dramatically transformed by the application of images. His decorative style was based on illusionism, architectural perspectives, and a host of personal leitmotifs, such as playing cards, the sun, the moon and classical images, from which he created seemingly endless variations. Fornasetti began experimenting with different printing techniques in the 1940s and developed a transfer technique for applying his designs to ceramics as well as his furniture. As collectors continue to appreciate Fornasetti's use of allusion, his striking images and surprising juxtapositions, his ceramics are delighting, shocking and inspiring as much as they did when they first appeared.

BELOW Mid-century faïence stoneware often had polychrome decoration over a white glaze. The rounded shapes and uneven rims of these hand-thrown vases have a subtle asymmetry. The tall vase was dabbed with watered-down pigments and then brushed with a black-brown iron glaze, the vase other with alternating sepia and ochre over a white body.

Roger Capron is one of the most esteemed mid-century ceramicists in France, where he is acclaimed for the artistic élan he added to the genre. His work contributed to the free-form movement in France and was strongly influenced by the cubism of Picasso. He often combined disparate elements and conflicting shapes, to create a sense of movement. Pigments and glazes were as important to him as form, and he restricted his colours to a single, distinctive palette, which assists authentication today.

In the 1950s the work of Europeans had a strong influence on North American ceramicists, who combined the elegant utility of Scandinavia with the spontaneity of France and Italy. Between the wars several influential European ceramicists relocated to the United States, where their techniques had great impact. The Austrians Otto and Gertrud Natzler established a studio in Los Angeles, where they continued producing work that brought them international recognition. The couple pioneered an understanding of beauty and materials based on spiritual awareness, and advocated a purist approach to form.

Otto and Vivika Heino set up their New England studio in the late 1940s, turning to European masters like the Natzlers for inspiration. Highly productive and successful, they received many awards. Otto's work demonstrates his eye for form and his ability to relate a vessel's surface design to its character and shape. Vivika's style was more delicate, and glazes were her forte. The rich pigments and grades of clay that the Heinos formulated can be found in almost every American ceramic laboratory today.

Gordon and Jane Martz established their studio in Indiana and developed a robust stoneware formula based on local clay. Their stoneware 'body' was well suited to mass production, and they pioneered a range of factory-produced items that had the characteristics of hand-thrown ceramics. The couple designed lamp bases that were slip-cast for mass production, but applied incised decorations by hand.

In California Barbara Willis also made major contributions to commercially produced ceramics. She had studied with the noted studio ceramicist Laura Anderson, whose hand-thrown work combined bisque and crackle-glazed clay. Using the same techniques, Willis cast her work in moulds. Her distinctive palette included turquoise, citron and Chinese red. The reappraisal of mid-century ceramics has made Willis's work more popular than ever, as it has the work of many leading ceramicists of the period.

ABOVE These two sauce boats were designed by Johan Verde for Figgjo in 2002, their unadorned surfaces and spare forms typical of his minimalistic style. Although they are contemporary, these pieces recall timeless classics such as Lindberg's Veckla.

RIGHT These Gaiety vases were produced in the early 1960s by Hornsea Pottery, which made some of the decade's most innovative ceramics. The company stopped trading in 2000, sparking renewed interest in collecting its vintage pieces.

LEFT The strict shapes of Kaj Franck's oeuvre distinguish it from the bulbous vessels of the 1950s. His Kartio pieces, shown here, are distinctive for their pure geometric shapes and translucent colours. All superfluous decoration was eschewed as he pursued minimal forms and timeless shapes.

RIGHT A 1950s icon, the Fazzoletto ('Handkerchief') vase, by Paolo Venini and Fulvio Bianconi, was reportedly inspired by a handkerchief floating through the air. Fazzoletto was produced in Murano by Venini, but the design was widely copied throughout the world in the 1950s.

FAR RIGHT Technical innovations enabled a deep ruby red, a colour previously derived from gold, to be produced in crystal by a relatively inexpensive method. The wide-rimmed crystal bowl was designed by Vicke Lindstrand while he was design director at Kosta Boda in Sweden.

Glass

The ongoing popularity of 1950s glass, once referred to as 'the collectables of the future', shows that it has lived up to its promise. Long-stemmed glasses, trumpet vases, scent bottles, sculptures and chandeliers were prized for their delicacy, while colourful paperweights, textured platters and imaginative tableware added an artistic dimension to utilitarian objects. As glass developed a new sculptural confidence, it revolutionized the production of everyday utensils and lent a dynamic beat to their surroundings.

Artists had begun to replace craftsmen as glass designers in the 1920s and '30s, and many manufacturers had divided their production into main lines of vases, wine glasses and tumblers, with separate studios for art glass. During the 1950s these divisions became more porous, with the swirling colours and breathtaking shapes pioneered in art glass mirrored in functional designs.

Paolo Venini was a Venetian glassmaker who had begun exploring the artistic potential of glass in 1921. His company in Murano became the leading Italian glass manufacturer, and he encouraged collaborations between artists and designers. Venini was celebrated for his unpredictable, asymmetrical forms and the sculptural dimension he pioneered in glass, contributing to the renaissance of Murano glass in the 1950s.

117

TOP LEFT Murano, a cluster of islands north of Venice, has been a centre of glass production since the fourteenth century. Italian glass then gradually declined till the twentieth century, when glassworks such as Venini, founded in 1921, revived the industry, followed in the 1940s by Barovier & Toso and Vistosi. The pieces shown here attest to the rich colours and striking shapes of Murano glass.

BOTTOM LEFT Vases blown in overlapping cubic shapes and dense bowls crafted in colourful crystal were popular throughout the 1950s. The tall vases shown here were created by folding molten glass into pressed forms, while low, rounded forms were shaped in a centrifuge.

RIGHT As this colourful mid-century glass captures the light, it creates a spectacular display.

Venini mentored glass artists such as Fulvio Bianconi, who had already designed glass figurines alongside Michaela Pinta before going to Murano. Bianconi imbued his work with verve, expressing his passion and energy in designs that featured multicoloured streams and original colour harmonies. Vibrant pieces such as his Pezzato vase (1951) banded bold stripes over geometric shapes, while his 1955 Attorcigliato series morphed soft colours into rippled textures. Bianconi had a predilection for figurative works, such as commedia dell'arte characters.

One of his friendly rivals was Dino Martens, who had a penchant for turning functional designs into sculptural objects that transcended function altogether. He crafted ewers with elongated spouts, looping their handles and spiralling their necks into extraordinary shapes, decorated with a fusion of lozenge-shaped fragments and filigree streaks melted into a smooth, opaque surface. His style was echoed in the work of Luciano Gaspari, whose free-form vessels seemed spontaneously to fragment into angular shapes recalling twisted metal.

Aldo Nason brought dynamism to Murano at a time when the industry had been criticized for becoming stagnant. His sculptural shapes were often inspired by organic forms, and his designs contrasted with the more subdued, elegant styles that had typified Murano during the pre-war era. Nason was inspired by shapes such as hollow tree trunks and fossilized teeth, which he adorned with a rainbow of candy-coloured motifs.

Flavio Poli's work expressed an aesthetic of simplified shapes and understated colours that was more akin to the designs of his Scandinavian counterparts than his fellow countrymen. Between 1950 and 1960 he developed a preference for 'cold' colours, elliptical forms and subtle, spherical silhouettes. Poli's series of Sommerso pieces, formed by fusing several layers of coloured glass together, suggested a Nordic influence, and some were awarded the prestigious Compasso d'Oro prizes.

Although their palettes were seldom as vibrant as the Italians', Scandinavian designers experimented with the effects of original colour pigments and the use of different additives in glass. At Orrefors, one of Sweden's most esteemed glassworks, the creative focus throughout the 1950s was directed by four young designers, Sven Palmqvist, Edvin Öhrström, Nils Landberg and Ingeborg Lundin. They developed colours and techniques that revolutionized the industry, with innovative designs that seemed to be sculpted with water, tinted with raw pigments or shimmering with an incandescent light emanating from the vessels' core. Using dense glass bodies, they cut motifs deep into the surface, producing pieces that resembled multi-faceted jewels.

Sven Palmqvist had begun to exploit the potential of coloured glass in the 1930s. In the late 1940s and '50s, inspired by the rich colours and patterns of Byzantine mosaics, he produced the Ravenna ranges, in which a mosaic effect was created by floating pieces of coloured glass within the vessels' dense walls.

Likewise, Edvin Öhrström suspended patterns and shapes between layers of clear glass. He developed the Ariel technique of sandblasting motifs into a clear glass plate before coating it with molten glass in a method that trapped pockets of air. By the 1950s, his technique was finding full expression in his sculptures and public works, but towards the end of the decade his simple works blown in crystal were also much admired.

Nils Landberg became known for abstract designs engraved on bulbous vases, which evolved into an acclaimed Tulip series of glasses with daringly long, thin stems and rounded bodies. Their beauty and delicacy earned them worldwide recognition. They were said to be the most difficult designs the glass-blowers had ever produced, but the results made it well worth the effort.

Ingeborg Lundin was a designer who never accepted the limitations of glass, becoming celebrated throughout the 1950s for sculptural pieces that pushed out the boundaries of the medium. In her hands, glass became a means of harnessing properties of light and transparency, which she highlighted with iridescent colours and elegant forms. Exemplifying her ability to capture the beauty of an everyday object in glass, Lundin's Apple vase of 1955 changed the way her generation saw the ordinary apple.

[While mid-century designers pared down the shapes of vases, serving vessels, tumblers and wine glasses, they also created art studios that enabled glass to attain a new sculptural confidence.]

Kosta Boda is Sweden's longest-surviving glassworks, but it often lagged behind Orrefors in its contemporary designs. In 1950 Vicke Lindstrand, the new artistic director, introduced several of the innovations he had developed while working at Orrefors. Lindstrand produced many key designs that took Kosta Boda forward, such as the Negress vase (1953), which he crafted in the elongated shape of a Ndebele tribeswoman's neck and head. His Trees in the Fog (1957) was another pivotal piece, depicting a spectral birch forest under glass.

In Norway, Lindstrand's approach was shared by Willy Johansson, who in 1958 became head of design at Hadeland, one of the country's oldest glassworks. Earlier he had been recognized for his ground-breaking work and awarded the Diplôme d'Honneur at the 1954 Milan Triennale. His skill and experience enabled him to achieve near-perfect symmetry in his free-blown designs, in hues that slowly intensified as he drew the pigments towards the outer edges, bordered with opaque rims. He also cast vases in wooden moulds and decorated them with cores of contrasting colours, then sandblasted them to lend a soft sheen.

Mid-century designs from Denmark's Holmegaard glassworks were characterized by simplicity, classical shapes and high-quality production. Under Per Lütken, the artistic director, the company introduced several influential ranges of contemporary glass in the 1950s. Among Lütken's best-known works are his Beak vases, Provence bowls and austere, one-off art-glass pieces. He was also behind many pioneering forms created by other designers and manufactured at Holmegaard, such as the double-walled Blue bowl by Henning Koppel (1958) and the opaline glass-and-wood range by Jacob Bang (1960).

In Finland the 1950s is remembered as a golden decade for the country's glass. Award-winning designers such as Tapio Wirkkala and Timo Sarpaneva, both based at Iittala, created several ranges of elegant and forward-thinking designs. Wirkkala produced a large body of work based on jagged ice blocks, lichen vessels and mushroom shapes, while his Tapio range of clear glassware (1954) captured the lightness and transparency of air, trapping an air bubble within each dense stem.

ABOVE Per Lütken was known for his distinctive undulating forms and preference for bodies of dense glass, and his designs reflect the understated organic shapes that characterized mid-century Danish glassware. Lütken's spare use of colour resulted in monochromatic hues of pale pastels or smoked glass, as well as vessels in clear crystal.

ABOVE RIGHT Classic 1950s motifs were used to decorate these twenty-first century tumblers, reviving the patterns that were etched into drinking glasses more than fifty years ago.

ABOVE FAR RIGHT In the late 1950s, Per Lütken began exploring cylindrical forms, and his bottle vases transformed a classic shape into colourful contemporary vessels.

Sarpaneva's work moved from functional efficiency to superfluous luxury and back again. During the mid-1950s he brought a sculptural approach to his i-Glass range of utility glassware, produced in smoky colours with a subtle metallic tint that caught the eye of other designers, creating one of the signature colour palettes of the 1950s. Centring around sculptural expression, his Lansetti vases of 1952 were bases on a void-like pocket of air encased within a solid crystal mass, while his Orchid vase of 1953 was formed by creating an empty well near the base of a dense glass monolith.

Parallel to his role at the ceramics factory Arabia, Kaj Franck designed glass for Nuutajärvi from 1950. Franck's approach to glass reflected the subtlety and restraint he introduced to ceramics, captured in glass tumblers and pitchers that echoed the clean lines of his Kilta ceramic service. Franck made a global contribution to the glassware industry while at Nuutajärvi, by developing a means of standardizing glass shapes and sizes in order to make them stackable.

Less well-known than Franck but just as significant, Göran Hongell produced simplified shapes that he seldom decorated. His Aarne glassware (1950) is still produced by Iittala. With their smooth, cylindrical bases they demonstrate the importance of glasses that are as pleasing to the touch as they are to the eye.

Metalware

LEFT Grete Prytz transformed functional metalware into an art form, creating bold graphic patterns outlined in vibrant colours. As durable as they are beautiful, her 1950s designs are often found in perfect condition after fifty years of use.

ABOVE Jens Quistgaard's Kobenstyle metalware coffee pot and milk pan were coated in turquoise enamel and furnished with a woven handle. The Kobenstyle range of cookware also functioned as elegant tableware.

ABOVE RIGHT These hammered aluminium pieces from Buehner-Wanner were popular throughout the 1940s, '50s and '60s. Those bearing the Buenilum mark or the BW castle-turret mark are originals.

Although the fragile arts of glass-blowing and ceramics yield works of unparalleled expression, the durability of metal means that metalwork designs are the longest-lasting. Mid-century designers therefore approached their craft with an awareness of the permanence of their work.

With the growing popularity of contemporary style, modern vessels crafted from stainless steel and chrome rivalled those made from silver and pewter, and were often combined with wood or other materials to provide practical utensils. From breakfast trays and toast racks to champagne coolers and cocktail shakers, colourful enamels, matt finishes and textured surfaces replaced the gleaming sheens of traditional materials and gave metalware a new look.

The ancient craft of metalwork was married to modern design practice in the 1950s by silversmiths such as Lino Sabattini who made full use of the technology that made it possible to manufacture fine silver objects industrially. New production techniques streamlined and simplified the casting process

but left little scope for aesthetically pleasing embellishments. Sabattini eschewed ornamentation, designing functional silver vessels crafted in undulating planes, whose unadorned surfaces gloried in the lustre of the material. Acclaimed for the sleek vessels and smooth trays he designed for tea and coffee services such as Boule (1950) and Como Tea (1956), Sabattini reinvented the shape of many essential service forms. In 1956, at the height of his career, he designed a silver coffee pot for Christofle that proved to be one of his seminal works, and it has since been acquired by museums and private collections around the world.

From his studio in Helsinki, the Finnish designer Bertel Gardberg produced numerous pieces of award-winning metalware from 1949 onwards. He introduced a new aesthetic based on cubic forms in his silver and teak tea range of the 1950s, and designed rippling, ring-shaped saucepans for his Canton series of cookware. Gardberg's silver tea caddy and chocolate pot flattened the rounded shapes of traditional pots into rectilinear planes that tapered upwards from the base, rounding the corners into gentle folds. Carelia, his stainless-steel cutlery (flatware) range of 1957, was produced in Finland and sold to an international market.

Piet Hein, the Danish designer, was actually a mathematician and a philosopher who found inspiration in the relationship between art and science for several metalware designs. His Great Bear stainless-steel candelabra (1944) was designed with arms that revolved like a stellar constellation to align seven candles into the astronomical configuration known as the Great Bear or the Big Dipper.

While Hein's colleague Arne Jacobsen is best known for his furniture and his architecture, the scope of his vision included candelabras among his many metalware designs. Jacobsen's silver-plated Spherical candlestick (1957) has been reintroduced by the silversmith Georg Jensen, along with the stainless-steel AJ cutlery that Jacobsen designed in the same year for the Royal Hotel, Copenhagen. This minimalist cutlery set was regarded as a vision of future aesthetics, and it was subsequently featured in Stanley Kubrick's film *2001: A Space Odyssey*.

Another Dane, the metalware designer Herbert Krenchel produced in 1953 the ubiquitous Krenit enamelled steel bowls, which are regarded today as a benchmark in household design. The bowls were machine-pressed from plates of thin steel and their interiors were enamelled in deep red, sky blue and off-white.

ABOVE LEFT Arne Jacobsen's aluminium candelabra is simple and elegant, making a style statement in any setting. Jacobsen interlinked three identical orbs so that the candelabra's circular design could be appreciated from any vantage point.

BELOW Arne Jacobsen designed the AJ stainless-steel cutlery set in 1957. Each piece fits naturally in the hand to give the user greater freedom and ease of movement. The striking minimalism of the cutlery was interpreted as an aesthetic so futuristic that it was chosen for use in Kubrick's film *2001, A Space Odyssey*. **RIGHT** Folke Arström's Focus de Lux cutlery set was crafted in stainless steel with Bakelite handles. **FAR RIGHT** Mid-century cutlery was expressive and sleek, heralding a new direction for domestic metalware.

LEFT Vertical stainless-steel cylinders replaced the bulbous silver bodies of previous decades. Here, a mid-century coffee pot and pitcher have been crafted in streamlined, imposing shapes that seemed futuristic at the time. The coffee pot was fitted with heat-resistant metal handles.

BELOW LEFT These capsule-shaped coffee pots were crafted in silver by Nick Monroe, and the handles bound with heat-resistant plastic.

RIGHT These coffee pots were designed by Robert Welch in 1957 for the Campden stainless steel tableware range.

Grete Prytz (later Grete Prytz Kittelsen) was also a leader in enamelled metalware, which she coloured in glossy primary hues and embellished with simple line drawings. She was based in Oslo, and her designs were manufactured by the Oslo silversmith Jacob Tostrup and sold internationally. Her enamelled steel tableware had a robust, masculine feel, while her cutlery reflected the same imposing elegance found in her enamelled jewellery.

Robert Welch, the celebrated British designer, had come across the works of Grete Prytz when working with the silversmith Theodor Olsen in Norway. Welch was clearly influenced by Scandinavian design in his functional precision and preference for clean lines. He first encountered modern stainless steel in Sweden during the war years, and he later pioneered the use of an equivalent material in Britain. Welch's cutlery, coffee pots and toast racks are now being hailed as design classics and are being snapped up in vintage shops and auction rooms. His commissions for Old Hall resulted in many timeless ranges, including sets of stainless-steel candlesticks, the Westclox alarm clocks and the Alveston cutlery set.

Welch co-designed the classic Campden cutlery set with David Mellor in 1958. Reputed to be the first modern cutlery in stainless steel produced in Britain, it is still manufactured today. Mellor designed the silver-plated Pride cutlery set in 1953, also acknowledged as a modern classic. He created the six-piece place settings when he was still a student at the Royal College of Art in London, and the range has been in production ever since. As their careers evolved, both Mellor and Welch were instrumental in bringing contemporary metalware styles to British homes.

[Mid-century designers of metalware approached their work with the knowledge that their enduring pieces were destined to become the artefacts of the future, as they outlive the fragile arts of ceramics and glass.]

Tableware

The spontaneous shapes and striking new silhouettes captured in art glass and in studio ceramics also found expression in everyday utensils. Modest household objects were influenced by curvaceous profiles and abstract forms, and modern tableware was seen as a vehicle for creative inspiration.

China sets, cutlery and serving dishes, as well as cruets, centrepieces and carafes, were often crafted into sculptural works that transcended notions of function and utility. The new designs reflected the changing look of the interior, stylishly incorporating the biomorphic designs and organic shapes that influenced the furniture, lighting and artworks of the period.

[During the 1950s, tableware took on a new, creative dimension as designers transformed functional utensils into sculptural expressions of modern style.]

North American designers produced some of the most innovative china and crockery of the 1950s, creating functional pieces that were beautiful enough to be placed on display rather than stowed away in a sideboard. Sasha Brastoff was one of the most celebrated American tableware designers of the time, and he created ranges of modern, exquisitely produced ceramic tableware, most of which was hand-crafted by his studio and signed personally. Brastoff's work was referred to as 'modern art pottery' during the 1950s, because of his unusual glazes, spectacular metallic colours and painterly motifs. He also created objects for the sideboard and the coffee table, designing china cigarette boxes and lighters, domed ashtrays and coasters.

Before settling in the United States, Hungarian-born Eva Zeisel had worked in Russia, Austria and England, where her European style had been influenced by the geometric designs of the Bauhaus and the abstract shapes of Jean (Hans) Arp. Zeisel possessed an instinctive understanding of how ceramics should communicate as an ensemble and how a dinner service could set the tone of a meal. From her first American commissions in the 1940s, she mapped out an elegant modern style that would appeal to homemakers until the early 1960s. Her tea sets, fruit bowls, storage containers and dinnerware forecast a new era of tableware and created interest in the creative potential of china.

The designs in Zeisel's Museum series (1946) were noted for their vertical profiles, which moved tableware away from traditional lateral forms. Museum was followed by the dynamic Town and Country dinner service (1946) for Red Wing Pottery. The series was reissued several decades later, and its elegant contours and looping handles continue to look strikingly contemporary. Zeisel went on to create the acclaimed Tomorrow's Classic series for Charles Seliger and her classic Bouquet series before retiring from commercial design in the mid-1960s.

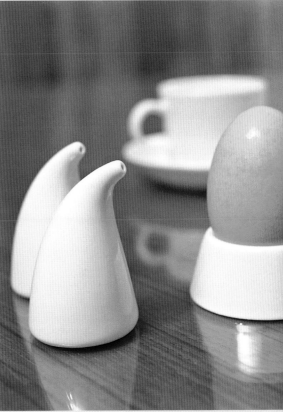

LEFT The durability of plastic has enabled melamine dinnerware to outlive many of its ceramic contemporaries. The dinner service on this table from Orbitin was made for use outdoors. It is shown with a melamine sugar bowl and creamer.

ABOVE RIGHT Almost every mid-century home owned a china tea or coffee service, which reflected the elegant contemporary style of the mid-century home.

RIGHT Kaj Franck designed these salt and pepper shakers in 1952 as part of his Kilta range of tableware. They were not designed as elements of the service but as individual pieces that would coordinate with Kilta's aesthetic.

Russel and Mary Wright promoted a new, informal way of living for suburban Americans. Their American Modern china set was stylish enough to suit formal occasions, yet practical enough for daily use. Produced in low-fired earthenware, American Modern was characterized by organic lines and graceful designs that were easy to care for and comfortable to use every day. American Modern included plates of different sizes, soup bowls, serving bowls, pitchers, sauce boats, 'hostess' serving platters, cups and saucers – each streamlined and set atop a rounded foot. American Modern is reportedly the best-selling dinnerware in American history, and it was reissued years later by Oneida, which remained faithful to the Wrights' original colours and glazes.

The Wrights produced American Modern in eleven colours: earthy tones evocatively named Bean Brown, Black Chutney, Granite Grey and Glacier Blue; and pastel colours described as Chartreuse Curry, Seafoam Blue, Coral, Cantaloupe, Cedar Green and Steubenville Blue (named after the range's manufacturer). White was also popular. The Wrights introduced their Iroquois range in 1946, which was available in fourteen colours. Aqua, Ice Blue, Parsley Green, Avocado, Pink Sherbet, Lettuce Green, Ripe Apricot, Cantaloupe, Nutmeg Brown, Oyster and Sugar White brought subtle tones to the American tabletop, while Brick Red, Charcoal and Lemon Yellow offered stronger hues.

Colours like these were also widely available in plastic, a material that had been engineered during the 1940s to be versatile, durable and unbreakable. Melamine became a miracle material in the hands of Russel Wright, who introduced the Residential range of plastic tableware in 1953. The range included sleek serving dishes and wide platters with curved rims, in which organic forms merged with electric colours. While Formica table-tops and work surfaces were popular in the mid-century home, many home-owners preferred tableware produced in natural materials – although they were never porous enough to retain the strong colour dyes that plastics could.

The Dansk brand of wooden tableware was co-founded by Jens Quistgaard in Denmark and Ted Nierenberg in the United States, where the range was enormously popular with the American public. Established in 1954, the industrially produced Dansk range appealed to those who revered natural materials

and was characterized by a hand-crafted touch. Pine cheeseboards, elm salad bowls, teak ice buckets, cedar boxes, and beech serving platters were crafted in designs that celebrated the natural beauty of wood.

British mid-century tableware is best remembered for ranges such as Homemaker (1955), with its distinctive pattern of black and white lines inset with drawings of boomerang-shaped tables, and chairs with pointed legs, as well as other illustrations of contemporary furnishings. Homemaker was designed by Enid Seeney for Ridgway Potteries and, uniquely, sold through Woolworth's until 1967.

Probably the most dynamic English manufacturer of the 1950s, Midwinter commissioned many leading artists and designers to produce fashionable tableware. Its spectacular Stylecraft range of tableware was manufactured throughout the 1950s in a selection of motifs, for which the company received international acclaim. Patterns such as Fiesta, Ming Tree and Primavera were designed by Jessie Tait, who had joined the company in the late 1940s. Hugh Casson designed the motifs for Riviera, featuring cameos of a summer holiday in the south of France, and other guest designers included the young Terence Conran, John Russell, David Queensberry and Peter Scott.

Tabletop combinations of fine china, earthenware, plastic and wood reflected a relaxed, informal approach to eating and dining, which attested to the changing lifestyles of mid-century homemakers. The mix-and-match style of table setting lent itself to intimate family suppers and formal dinner parties, and gave the hosts an opportunity to display their collection of contemporary objects. As mid-century tableware continues to adorn the tabletops of the twenty-first century, the icons of the 1950s keep the spirit of casual dining alive.

LEFT Many of the Swedish ceramicist Stig Lindberg's tableware designs were crafted in contouring shapes that resembled leaves, while many others featured repeating leaf motifs. Here, Lindberg simplified the outline of leaves into triangular shapes and drew their veins as parallel lines.

ABOVE Midwinter ceramic tableware was fired in Britain but sold widely in North America. The contrasting black and white lines and red accents of Jessie Tait's Zambesi pattern bespoke the new graphic language that characterized mid-century ceramics.

MID-CENTURY STYLE

Considering that the style evolved amid scepticism that it was merely a passing trend, the popularity of 1950s décor is truly remarkable, as these mid-century interiors demonstrate.

Mid-century modernism was never masterminded with a grand unifying vision, but evolved organically as it spread across the globe through European triennales, travelling exhibitions and Hollywood films, eventually redefining local design traditions and creating a market for imported designs. Mid-century pieces represented something that was truly universal, and they united different worlds by establishing an international visual language. Every new product seemed to carry the spirit of optimism, and they charged every household with the promise of a better future.

Today mid-century décor seems at once sophisticated and subversive as it combines a deep appreciation for classical design with a subtle disregard for the stranglehold of trend-based products. Part of the style's appeal is the flexibility with which it can exist harmoniously alongside furniture from other periods. As it can intermingle with modernist pieces from the 1930s, the pop art movement of the 1960s, the indulgent designs of the 1970s and the austere minimalism that dominated the 1990s, it successfully bridges the gap between high aesthetics and popular taste. Mid-century décor is also very much at home with a wide variety of architectural traditions, ranging from the period interiors of the early Victorian era to the box-like rooms of the 1970s and the vast loft spaces of the 1990s.

These unique syntheses of styles are given a twenty-first century context as this chapter takes an inside look at six interior design schemes of mid-century enthusiasts. Each example reveals a different aspect of mid-century style, shaped by climate and geography as much as personal taste.

The versatility and internationalism of the style become apparent as continental chic is contrasted with British restraint, and Northern European sensibilities are juxtaposed with the laid-back, indoor-outdoor lifestyle associated with southern California. Scandinavian designs provide stunning accents in Californian homes, and American designs, originally devised with the moderate West Coast climate in mind, harmonize with Nordic décor in a Swedish interior.

In the rolling hills of England, the countryside home of a leading architect and his wife proved to be one of Britain's most original mid-century properties. The couple, remarkably, have been living in the same, immaculate interior for nearly fifty years without redecorating or introducing any significant changes. An architectural masterpiece, the house was designed in the mid-1950s and completed in 1961, demonstrating the extent to which mid-century principles underpinned many homes of the 1960s. Also considered a masterpiece, a luxurious house in Palm Springs was designed by Richard Neutra, a Viennese émigré who inspired the mid-century architectural style that flourished on the American West Coast. The home fell into disrepair, and the monumental task of restoration and redecoration was taken on by a young couple determined to return the house to its former glory.

Not every mid-century enthusiast can claim to live in an architectural gem, and many people enjoy the clean start provided by a newly built home. In Stockholm the penthouse apartment of a leading mid-century dealer boasts an unrivalled collection of 1950s treasures, each expertly restored to its original splendour. In London a Victorian apartment in the heart of the sprawling metropolis is an equally unlikely backdrop for 1950s designs, but the owner has filled his home with robust, sculptural pieces that contrast with the period features rather than clashing with them. Like his fellow enthusiast in Sweden, the British collector has an eye for rare finds, and each one is in perfect condition. His elegant apartment delights in a compellingly eclectic décor, which is nevertheless also restrained and masculine.

Los Angeles is known for its steep canyons and tiny residential plots in the flatlands, but few denizens realize the architectural significance of its geography. Grounding houses in a sloping terrain or cantilevering them off steep hillsides has necessitated a split-level style, and the need to create privacy within close confines has inspired walled gardens and secluded central courtyards. A split-level house built around a courtyard here provides a dramatic backdrop for a growing collection of furniture by mid-century American designers.

Renewed appreciation of styles of 1970s domestic architecture is sweeping Northern Europe, and many 1970s homes are decorated in a variety of retro styles, ranging from the late 1940s to the late 1970s. One such house is owned by a mid-century dealer and her architect husband, who use the interior to showcase the items they sell from home. The interior of the couple's house changes constantly, just as any retail showroom would, and as they combine, contrast and clash furniture from different periods their home reveals the versatility of the mid-century look.

These homes belong to young families, middle-aged couples and single people, who create environments for living, working, entertaining and simply relaxing. Each home exposes a different appreciation of mid-century living and a different approach to decorating the interior, but all reveal the timelessness and adaptability of a style that remains strikingly contemporary today.

AN ARCHITECTURAL IDYLL

A meandering gravel drive winds its way between colossal fir trees and rustic cottages before meeting the smooth outdoor terraces of one of Britain's most spectacular mid-century homes. At the outermost reaches of a historic village and skirting the tranquil woods and gentle hills of the English countryside, the house brings the modernist style to life in an unexpected milieu. Undaunted by the pastoral surroundings, the architect and his wife set out to express a new look for the British home that would appeal in any landscape.

The couple designed the house as a family home where they would bring up their two young children, and they have changed very little in the interior since they moved in almost five decades ago. Although sketches for the house were begun in 1956, it took almost five years to construct, complete, furnish and decorate the home. The orientation of the rooms, and the relationships between them, was considered innovative and unique at the time, as the design of the house enabled it to grow with the family, yet ensured seamless continuity between all areas when completed.

The first phase created a compact nucleus of eight rooms on the upper level of the house, with only a glazed entrance hall, cloakroom (powder room) and garage on the ground floor. The structural walls were constructed in buff-coloured Woodham bricks, chosen for their pale colours and smooth finishes. As the walls extended upwards through the core of the house, their exposed brickwork made richly textured backdrops in the living areas. On the ground floor the structural walls merged with sheets of plate glass to create the entrance hall and cloakroom, then angled into the garden to form boundary walls and a protective barrier for the shallow pool. The central structural wall acted as an architectural 'spine' running through the core of the building, as if suspending the upper floor over the garden. Load-bearing brick walls at either end of the house functioned as supports for the upper floor and were eventually integrated into the interior scheme as the house grew.

LEFT In the kitchen, cabinet doors were coated with white plastic laminate in order to contrast with the teak woodwork and lighten the look.

BELOW LEFT This stainless-steel Oriana coffee service has been in continuous use since it was designed by Robert Welch in 1958.

THIS PAGE The breakfast bar was a standard feature in mid-century kitchens, but here it was conceived as a room divider and a serving buffet to maximize its functionality.

ABOVE A series of sliding doors in the master bedroom suite eliminates the need for a hallway. Full-height sliding doors rolled into the partition walls open up the area and channel sunlight through the core of the home.

ABOVE RIGHT The long dining table is flanked on both sides by teak dining chairs with seats crafted from woven piping cord. The sideboard was custom-built with a hotplate and generous buffet area.

RIGHT A circular Eames coffee table stands on a flokati rug between two modernist sofas imported from Germany, and a pair of low basket stools are drawn close to the table's edge. The windows are dressed with light-coloured sheers.

FAR RIGHT An armchair and footstool from the Eames Aluminum Group, designed in 1956, are placed close to the built-in hi-fi system and TV console. The speakers were built directly into the wall and covered with circular mesh screens, seen behind the chair.

The upper floor was conceived as a modular space, divided by structural walls and subdivided by sliding doors and partitions into areas for living, sleeping and dining. The architect was determined to incorporate as much furniture into the fabric of the house as possible in order to streamline the use of space.

The single beds in the children's rooms were conceived as bunks rather than as free-standing beds and were built into the interior architecture along with desks and wardrobes. All this built-in furniture, in common with cupboards, work surfaces and woodwork, was crafted in teak.

As sunlight streams through the plate-glass walls, it gives the opaque floor tiles a glossy shimmer, making the floor appear translucent in places. In each room the mosaic tiles give way to aluminium vents set flush with the flooring, concealing the heating ducts incorporated into the floor's structure. These mosaic tiles were used throughout the upper-floor living space to pave the entire area in a seamless surface that provided a visual link between each room.

Most of the lighting features were designed as integral parts of the structure, arranged to complement the rectilinear lines of the house. Long, lateral cavities in the ceiling run the length of the rear exterior wall and trace the internal walls that separate the central corridor from the living areas. Fluorescent bulbs are concealed in the hollows overhead, eliminating the glare of a naked bulb and minimizing shadows as they soften and diffuse the light. Light fixtures in the living areas and bedrooms suspend pendant lamps or cast a concentrated spotlight beam directly downwards. In the kitchen the lighting was integrated into the cabinets to provide intense illumination over the work surfaces.

The owners' classic mid-century furniture, timeless textiles and unadorned tableware look as though they were purchased recently. Just as the house is undeniably contemporary today,

[Rather than decorate with wallpaper and paint finishes that need renewal over time, the brick walls and teak panelling were chosen for their enduring surfaces.]

it has had the same modern feel ever since it was designed. The owners attribute this to their choice of high-quality materials and the expertise of the craftsmen they commissioned to carry out the work. The durable waxed teak that lines the ceilings and walls and the hard-wearing glass tiles used in the mosaic floor have not needed the constant renewal required by paint finishes, wallpaper and vinyl flooring.

The same decorative devices were repeated in extensions made to the house in the next decade. As the children grew up, their small bedrooms were dismantled and incorporated into the dining area, which opened into a newly built wing of three bedrooms. Down below, most of the ground-floor terraces were enclosed by plate-glass and brickwork walls leading into a workroom, a storage area and a self-contained unit for visiting guests. Nearly fifty years later, the couple still enjoy the perfect house they set out to achieve half a century ago, impressively untouched by the passage of time.

FAR LEFT The 1950s bed has storage in the steel and plywood base, with steel tripod legs. A Robin Day armchair for Hille is just visible.

LEFT This part of the terrace was eventually enclosed, but the glass walls permit wide vistas over the garden.

THIS PAGE The entry hall assembles the key materials used in the house's construction: the black-painted steel of the staircase was also used in the exterior, the plate-glass windows are set in anodized aluminium frames, the floor is polished Portland stone and the walls Woodham brick. The Jacobsen armchair was made in 1955 in laminated beech, lacquered in black, with nickel-coated steel rods.

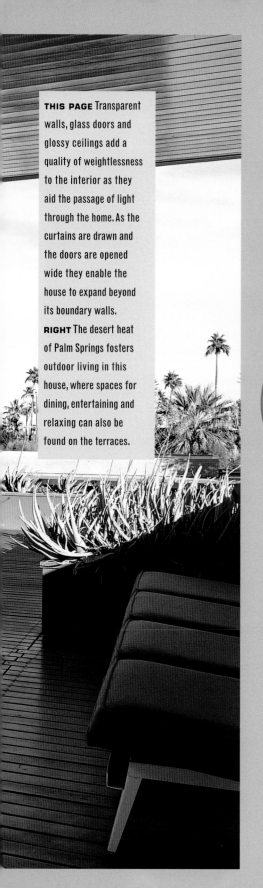

THIS PAGE Transparent walls, glass doors and glossy ceilings add a quality of weightlessness to the interior as they aid the passage of light through the home. As the curtains are drawn and the doors are opened wide they enable the house to expand beyond its boundary walls.
RIGHT The desert heat of Palm Springs fosters outdoor living in this house, where spaces for dining, entertaining and relaxing can also be found on the terraces.

02 PALM SPRINGS STYLE

A small settlement built near the point where the Colorado Desert and Mojave Desert meet might sound a highly unlikely oasis of modernist architecture, but Palm Springs is a stronghold of mid-century style that is unparalleled elsewhere in the world. During its heyday the town was regarded as a Hollywood playground, a golf mecca and a jet-set resort, but more recently Palm Springs has become renowned for the houses built by master architects such as Richard Neutra, William Cody, John Lautner and R M Schindler.

Verdant aquifers and luscious landscaped terraces have transformed the town into a garden of scented flowers where the eponymous palm trees thrive and fruit trees flourish. The surrounding desert scenery endows the town with spectacular views. The San Jacinto Mountains rise to the west, the Santa Rosas loom in the southern distance and the Little San Bernadino Mountains hover to the north. As the day passes, light and shadow change the face of these peaks, playing with the azure blue of the sky and the purple tints of the late afternoon.

It was the stunning landscape that drew a Los Angeles couple to Palm Springs at weekends, and they eventually bought and restored an iconic mid-century house designed by Richard Neutra in 1946. Originally built as a weekend playhouse for a business tycoon, the stone, aluminium and glass structure had been remodelled and extended over the years, and the original landscaped garden had been razed.

As architects and preservationists restored the house, landscape designers replanted the gardens with native Joshua trees, cholla cacti, palms, yucca, jojoba and creosote plants.

Neutra's distinctive reductive style eliminated interior walls and cut away ceilings, creating open-plan areas that afforded views over several rooms in a single visual sweep. Likewise, generous windows were fitted to overlook the surrounding landscape, drawing the house closer to the world beyond its walls. Neutra characteristically avoided sash or casement windows where possible, preferring to use single panels of glass that would flood the interior with light. Materials like redwood, teak and oak were used in the facade as well as in the interior architecture, further linking the exterior with the living space.

The restoration work took five years to complete, and during that time the couple, with their two daughters, visited the house every other weekend, watching the workmen turn back the wheels of time. As the house's period features were meticulously restored, the magical rhythm of Neutra's cubic asymmetry emerged. When the plate-glass windows were uncovered and the central core returned to its original proportions, the inflow of light from the outside and the vistas over the desert re-established the original relationship between the house and the landscape. Neutra's design enabled each part of the house to harness light from all points of the compass, ingeniously maximizing the amount of daylight shining in through the windows.

While the décor of the house is true to the minimalism advocated by Neutra, the owners have combined their classic furniture with rich colours and warm textures, which are well suited to the natural elements featuring in the interior architecture. The honey-coloured hues of the cork flooring and the blond tints of the plywood wall units and built-in daybeds harmonize with the earth tones and natural textures of the upholstery fabric and the patterned carpets.

The warm, dry desert climate means that the house's living spaces are not limited to areas contained behind walls. Open terraces surround the bedrooms and the living zones, where sliding glass doors can be pulled aside to allow the interior to spill outside. Neutra designed retractable aluminium louvres that could be rotated to shield the outdoor living area from the desert's fierce midday heat and also to protect it from driving windstorms. At night the stars in the desert sky sparkle as far as the eye can see, and the constellations seem no more distant than the horizon. Dazzling at night, the stone, glass and metal of the house's structure seem to transform it into a jewelled pavilion that mirrors the shimmering brilliance of the stars.

[Panels of glass replace exterior walls, and as the house fills with natural light its structure melts away, merging it with the desert beyond.]

RIGHT The dining area features classic Eames DCM chairs, designed in 1958, with rosewood seats and backrests. Their simplified structure echoes the sleek design of the table, while their curving outlines soften the parallel lines and right angles of the table.
BELOW The bathrooms were built en suite. Formica, plywood and cork were the standard materials of West Coast bathrooms, where china sinks and bathtubs were often surrounded by ceramic tiles.

The owners restored the swimming pool, a large tiled rectangle encased by a poured-concrete patio that gives way to the sloping green of the neat lawn. A new poolhouse was built on the foundation of Neutra's original clubhouse. It now contains a sauna lined in redwood panels and also a small gym where the owners can enjoy a workout in the cool atmosphere while looking out over the desert heat. With a golf course and tennis courts only a stone's throw away, the house can feel like a weekend resort as much as it does a desert retreat.

Today the house functions as an intimate family environment while serving as a pristine monument to mid-century modernism. As young couples, retired seniors or enlightened locals restore their towns' 1950s houses to their former glory, the movement is catching on in other American cities. But however spectacular their modernist buildings may be, few cities can hope to rival Palm Springs as the capital of mid-century style.

ABOVE The spacious kitchen is wider than those in most Neutra homes — he would typically design a narrow galley kitchen that had either a breakfast bar or a small dining nook at one end.

RIGHT This vista over the open-plan living area demonstrates that built-in furniture and free-standing pieces can work well together. The daybed, which is anchored in place by a plywood frame that matches the built-in wall unit, is paired with a coffee table in a similar-coloured veneer.

03 SWEDISH MODERN

The 1950s was a golden era in Sweden, when the country's architects, interior designers, textile artists, glass-blowers and furniture-makers forged an influential style. Although their works were sometimes known abroad as merely 'Scandinavian', the impact that Swedish designers had on other traditions was considerable. While Swedish mid-century designs are enjoying a renaissance abroad, in Sweden 1950s classics have never dated or fallen out of favour.

Few homes in Stockholm, built across an archipelago, are far away from the water, and many also overlook wooded parks or landscaped gardens. It comes as no surprise, then, that when Stockholm's leading mid-century dealer decided to sacrifice his period apartment for a bigger home for his growing family, he and his wife prioritized views of nature and more light along with more space. When they discovered a newly built top-floor apartment with outdoor terraces, breathtaking views and spacious, open-plan rooms, they moved in almost immediately, taking their mid-century décor with them.

Against such a pristine backdrop, the owners' cherished mid-century pieces suddenly looked tired. They considered investing in contemporary designs that would match their new home, but they realized that this furniture was not suited to their style. However, rather than redecorating the interior with modernist colours and mid-century motifs, they resolved their dilemma by making very subtle changes to their existing pieces. Worn cupboards, sagging shelving, faded rugs and scratched surfaces were ruthlessly ousted and replaced with items that had been meticulously restored, or well maintained in their original condition. An immaculate teak wall unit, superbly crafted

LEFT Produced by ViBi of Turin, this uniquely sculptural form looks like an artwork, but the openings on each side are clues that it was designed as a vase.

THIS PAGE A sideboard displaying ceramics and glassware by legendary Swedish designers is a striking backdrop for the sweeping contours of this chair and sofa.

ABOVE Routed patterns decorate the door panels of this classic sideboard.

RIGHT Rustic ceramics by Berndt Friberg and Stig Lindberg are displayed on this teak wall unit. On the left, simple bottle vases by John Selbing for Orrefors seem to crystallize the fiery glow of molten glass, while the lower shelves showcase a colourful range of beautiful opaque designs. The enamelled metalware bowls, which were made in Norway, are designed to nest inside the largest bowl.

TOP FAR RIGHT Like the canvas and moulded-plywood design of the classic Eames eight-panel screen, this pine room divider is easily rolled into a cylinder for storage.

BOTTOM FAR RIGHT The contrast of glossy black and white creates a dramatic dining suite.

[The brand-new interior was furnished with re-editions and vintage pieces that had been meticulously restored.]

by William Watting, an American designer, provided the perfect display case for the owners' treasure trove of rare ceramics, glass and metalware. In the spacious central corridor, the colourful objects can now be appreciated from the kitchen, dining area, bedrooms and entry hall. Practical items are stored in the commanding sideboard further down the hallway, hidden behind exquisitely carved teak doors.

The couple's bedroom could be mistaken for a guest room at first, as it is startling to come across a master bedroom where wardrobes, cupboards, clothing and personal accessories are absent. The bedroom was planned with minimalism in mind to provide an understated sleeping space where the owners could enjoy a sense of peaceful relaxation, and consequently a small room next door was converted into a dressing room with wardrobe. The bed itself is a simple plinth-like sprung base covered in dark fabric, which contrasts perfectly with the mid-century motif that inspired the contemporary Swedish bed linen. As the bed was not suited to a conventional headboard, a wooden screen was placed behind it. Two Norwegian tray-tables, chosen for their minimal design and squat proportions, completed the bedroom suite with a note of glossy colour.

Rather than replace their living-room furniture, the owners decided to update the fabrics, and reupholstered their capsule-shaped Capri couch and armchair, designed by Johannes Andersen for Trensum, in grey chenille. The original patterned fabric covering the Arabesque lounge chair by Folke Jansson was made into cushions, and the chair was reupholstered in yellow and black fabrics. The black Superellipse dining table was polished to a high gloss, and the limited-edition Jacobsen chairs – a rare find – were revamped with a white lacquer finish. While almost every item in the apartment has a twenty-first century vibe, its décor remains rooted in the mid-twentieth century as ageless classics are updated with contemporary style.

THIS PAGE In the interior the use of symmetry creates impact. This wall hanging, sideboard and tufted carpet seem to divide the space as a fusion of vibrant colour and rich textures sweeps through the centre of the room. The placement of the Diamond chairs by Harry Bertoia on either side enhances the effect.
RIGHT The eclectic juxtaposition of this sculptural pendant lamp with Victorian profile mouldings results in an eye-catching feature.

04

A LONDON INTERIOR

London interiors have always had a unique character, whether antique furniture is fast-forwarded into a twenty-first century setting, or a period interior is contrasted with ultra-contemporary refurbishments. Yet few homes dare to juxtapose the interior architecture of the 1850s with the understated style of the 1950s, as in this chic apartment that bridges a gap of a hundred years while adhering to the decorative principles that characterized both eras. Unvarnished wooden furniture and hand-loomed carpets blend perfectly into the period background of hardwood flooring, whitewashed walls and painted woodwork, all consistent with the stylistic vocabulary of the mid-nineteenth century.

The apartment, which is located in London's Notting Hill neighbourhood, stretches across two floors of a five-storey Victorian town house that is divided into separate apartments. Elevated high above the noise of the street, it overlooks a spectacular Georgian manse set within a walled garden. By purchasing the apartment shortly after conversion of the building had begun, the owner was able to ensure that the interior's historic features were preserved, while the living space was modernized and revamped.

The owner is a mid-century enthusiast, and everything he has gathered around him bears witness to his appreciation of the clean lines of 1950s design. Since he spends most of the week in a country house, where he lives with his wife and children, he wanted this to be an urban *pied à terre* where he could work from home in streamlined,

FAR LEFT Cowhides are making a comeback as mid-century décor becomes more popular. Paired with this striking Butterfly chair designed by the Argentinians Antonio Bonet, Jorge Ferrari-Hardoy and Juan Kurchan, it looks sensuous and appealing.

LEFT The abstract patterns of Terence Conran's Formica coffee table proclaim a colourful graphic statement that still resonates today.

RIGHT This sideboard was made with cupboards for storing china and tableware and drawers for holding linen and cutlery. The simple orb light on its top is a contemporary classic made in the spirit of Lisa Johansson-Pape's collection of round lamps designed in 1954. The earthenware piece to its right is both a functional object and an *objet d'art*. The chair is from Arne Jacobsen's Series 7 range, variants of his Ant chair of 1952.

efficient surroundings and still entertain guests and business colleagues in style. His decorating scheme came together quickly as he scoured furniture markets for mid-century furniture and bought key pieces from dealers in London's East End. Because beds, dining tables and comfortable sofas were at that time in short supply among 1950s specialists, he ordered these items from leading furniture shops instead, choosing ultra-contemporary pieces that mimicked mid-century modernism.

In a compact space where the entrance hall opens onto the living room, dining room and kitchen, a double-length desk, bookshelves and drawer units were built into a wide alcove under the stairs. Although in the core of the apartment, this area is filled with natural light streaming through the doorways and shining down from the landing. Two vintage Jacobsen chairs function as desk chairs, conversing fluently with the other mid-century pieces visible through the doorways around them.

The living room, which opens into the dining room and the entrance hall, spans the width of the apartment. Along the far wall, floor-to-ceiling windows open onto a small balcony. The white paint on the walls reflects light towards the core of the home as it highlights the living room's glossy surfaces. The room is crowned by a magnificent

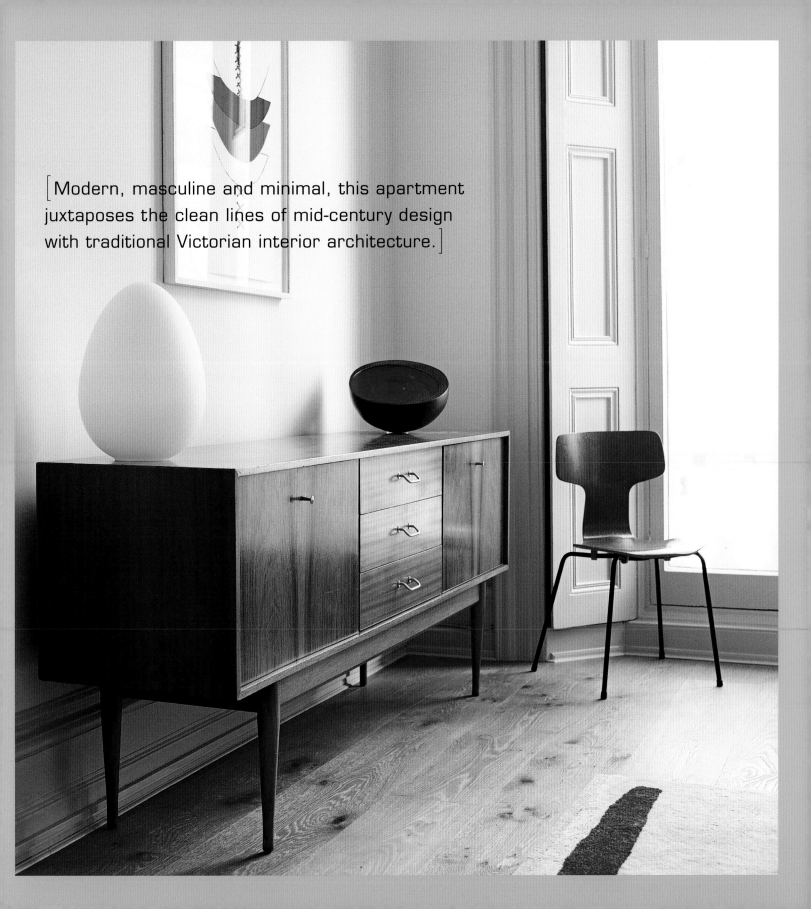

[Modern, masculine and minimal, this apartment juxtaposes the clean lines of mid-century design with traditional Victorian interior architecture.]

THIS PAGE On this moulded-plywood Cherner armchair designed by Paul Goldman in 1957, thin strips of wood twist and bend as they loop around its back and fasten underneath its base.

RIGHT The simple shapes of 1950s furniture and pieces inspired by mid-century aesthetics look striking in any setting. Although the minimalist style of these pieces creates strong silhouettes, they do not compete with the elaborate interior architecture around them.

spiral pendant lamp, in which plastic monofilament is woven onto a plastic-coated wire frame. The designer is unknown, but the shape is typical of lighting created by Desmond Sawyer in Britain, or the sculptural masterpieces by Ateljé Lyktan in Sweden.

The living room's cool white backdrop is tempered by a stunning geometric wall hanging hung above a burl-veneered sideboard. The sideboard is flanked by a pair of Harry Bertoia's Diamond chairs of 1952, providing a sculptural sweep of orange ochre at each end. The pair of wire-frame lamps placed near the ends recall the ubiquitous Akari lamps designed by Isamu Noguchi during the 1950s. Across the room a neutral, well-stuffed twenty-first century sofa sits between two windows, acting as a perfect foil for the colourful Formica coffee table designed by Terence Conran in the 1950s.

In the dining room classic Cherner dining chairs by the American designer Paul Goldman surround a steel and glass table designed in 2000 by Studio Archirivolto. Although Goldman designed the chairs in 1957, they look as fresh today as they did a half-century ago. Paired with the glass table, the sculptural beauty of the bentwood chairs can still be appreciated when the seats are beneath the table's surface. The room is illuminated by a colourful enamelled version of the Sputnik light fixture, centred over the dining table but casting beams of light in every direction. The light fixture is fitted with everyday bulbs that are easier to replace than the specialist crystal bulbs manufactured for the original brass-plated model.

In the master bedroom upstairs, the masculine lines of the simple, low wooden bedroom suite are contrasted against the wavy figure of an original Butterfly chair – officially known as the Hardoy Lounge Chair – which was updated with a leather sling when its original canvas sling started to fade. Combined with the curvy outline of a Brazilian cowhide rug imported from Denmark, it adds up to a characteristically sculptural mid-century silhouette that never seems to date. Like the Victorian setting in which they find themselves, their classic materials and expressive design will continue to be much appreciated for another hundred years.

05 LOS ANGELES MINIMALISM

Los Angeles, the capital of laid-back living, is known for its sun-drenched skies, palm-fringed gardens and Santa Ana winds that blow inland from the Pacific. The moderate climate promotes a unique indoor-outdoor lifestyle that makes California the envy of the rest of North America. Added to that, Los Angeles is a haven for 1950s architecture: Case Study houses (see page 18) were introduced there before spreading to other cities, and many leading mid-century designers designed homes in Beverly Hills, Bel Air, the Hollywood Hills and Brentwood.

Los Angeles is also known for its highly priced real estate, which for decades has been divided up into small plots or narrow tracts of land. When the architect Richard Neutra was commissioned to design a house for a tapering canyon slope in 1959, he conceived it as two interconnected structures rotated 30 degrees away from each other. By angling the house around a central courtyard and taking the structure close to the boundary walls, he maximized the amount of patio space in the courtyard, which was then naturally secluded from neighbouring homes. Almost every room on the ground floor opens onto the patio, enabling the owners to step out into a wonderfully light, tranquil space that is completely open to the sky. Planted simply with cacti, variegated grasses, aloes and other succulent plants, the quiet courtyard is the essence of the house's indoor-outdoor focus.

The U-shaped living area encircles the courtyard on three sides, set behind walls of plate glass bordered by sliding glass doors. Although this living space is open plan, it is cleverly zoned, with separate areas at either end for gathering in

LEFT Designed by Richard Neutra in 1959, the overhanging roof is cantilevered over the structure, supported by an exposed frame that extends into the garden. Parts of the split-level house are on stilts while others are bordered by a low retaining wall.

THIS PAGE Conventional partition walls are not found in this home, enabling separate living spaces to merge together. Instead of solid outer walls, plate-glass windows open up the exterior, and sliding glass doors glide aside to invite the garden in.

ABOVE The design is split-level, and the upper floor is accessed by a half-flight of stairs. This corridor staircase is atypical of mid-century homes, which usually featured open-tread staircases or spirals.

ABOVE RIGHT The vented construction of the roof overhanging the courtyard enables the house to adjust to the growth of the tree, which provides shade from the harsh midday sun.

RIGHT The den is a treasure trove of mid-century American classics, exemplifying the West Coast modernist style. The built-in desk is paired with a moulded-plywood DCW chair designed by the Eames in 1947, while Saarinen's Tulip chairs and dining table sit beneath George Nelson's Bubble lamp.

[The core of the home was conceived as a light-filled, tranquil terrace that opens to the sky above.]

front of the fireplace in the evenings or relaxing in the den and watching television. The flat, stacked bricks of the fireplace adjoin the room's outside walls and demarcate a smooth hearth set flush with the floor. The overhanging chimney breast is abutted by a single steel support that extends from floor to ceiling, echoing the structural framework that remains visible alongside the house's exterior, supporting its flat roof.

A half-flight corridor staircase cuts a passage to the next floor, which, because of the sloping landscape, is higher than the main part of the house. The bedroom suites are on this level, where they access a sundeck on the flat roof above the living room, and have a panoramic view over the patios below.

Back on the ground floor, the plywood wall units in the den provide an abundance of workspaces, display surfaces and shelves for books. The Saarinen dining table is a favourite spot for the children to do their homework after school, and it was moved closer to the bookcases so that they could make full use of the family's library. Sleek plywood surfaces also feature in the kitchen, where built-in units and cupboard doors were varnished in a glossy finish that shimmers in the passing light now just as it did more than fifty years ago. The stainless-steel kitchen appliances are hard-wearing vintage pieces that continue to function perfectly, and the current residents reckon they will see out another fifty years.

The owners are building their collection of mid-century furniture slowly, concentrating mostly on American designers including Eames, Noguchi, Saarinen and Nelson. The Danish designer Arne Jacobsen's Egg chair is the odd one out in their collection, but it suits the style of this American house as well as it does Danish homes. The Egg chair was inherited from the previous owners, who did not have space for it in their new place. As with the vintage kitchen appliances, its new guardians expect that it will still look great many years from now.

ABOVE RIGHT The galley kitchen was designed with space for state-of-the-art appliances and an abundance of storage. The glossy finish of the cabinets and the stainless-steel appliances reflect the light flooding in, making the compact space seem larger than it is.

RIGHT The single bunks in the children's rooms were built into the interior architecture along with shelves, wardrobes and writing desks. During the space craze of the 1950s, a vogue for rockets, comets and spaceships took hold, which clearly continues in the present day.

THIS PAGE Rooms in 1970s houses typically resemble white cubes, but their streamlined surfaces, sliding glass doors and wood flooring recall 1950s architecture. Their interiors offer an appropriate setting for the era's furniture.

RIGHT Soft furnishings create a comfort zone in any interior. Here, a contemporary couch is upholstered in taupe fabric and complemented by cushions made in Aristidia (left) and Celotocaulis (right) fabrics by Josef Frank.

06 THE RETRO HOME

In Northern Europe mid-century enthusiasts frequently have a penchant for 1970s architecture, where they can live in minimalist houses evoking the structural simplicity of mid-century homes. The interior architecture of the 1970s tended to be streamlined and somewhat stark, conceived as a series of white boxes rather than open areas separated by wood panelling, stone walls and other natural elements. But because many 1970s houses feature open-tread staircases, sliding glass doors, casement windows and angled rooftops characteristic of 1950s architecture, they often provide an ideal backdrop for mid-century furniture.

One 1970s architectural style that is still appreciated today is the type of residential estate designed by the British architect Ralph Erskine in 1956. In 1959 Erskine built his first residential model in Sweden, from where it spread to Finland, Belgium, The Netherlands, Britain and Ireland as it was imitated by other architects in the 1960s and 1970s. The estates are typically composed of two- and three-storey houses encircling a warren of low terraces and efficient bungalows separated by gardens, walkways and landscaped areas. The house featured here was built in the 1970s, and was purchased in 2002 by an architect and a journalist searching for their first family home. Inspired by the combination of compact living spaces and friendly, child-centred surroundings, they knew that the house would suit them perfectly.

Shortly after moving in with her husband and toddler, the owner drifted into dealing in vintage furniture as she sought to combine her love of classical design with her decision to work from home. She began furnishing the house with Saarinen tables, Tulip chairs, rare pieces from Scandinavian designers such as Arne Jacobsen, Jens Quistgaard, Finn Juhl and Hans Wegner, textiles from Josef Frank and popular designs by Charles and Ray Eames. Her husband is a fellow mid-century addict, who also scouts for bargains and helps organize practical aspects of the venture. The house provided the perfect showcase for the couple's design treasures, enabling them to live in style

and sell their finds without opening a separate shop. Because the pieces were sold from a living space, it was easier for clients to envisage how they would relate to other household accessories and gauge how they would suit their own homes. As the business began to grow, a partnership was established with another dealer, extending the showroom concept beyond the home as they set up regular mid-century trade fairs that brought dealers and collectors together.

A double set of sliding glass doors in the living room opens onto a wide patio overlooking a walled garden. Almost all the tables and chairs in the room are crafted with narrow pedestal bases or tapering legs, allowing light to pass beyond their structure and most of the floor area to remain in view. This bestows a greater sense of space than boxy furniture would, and also acts as a visual link between contrasting shapes and styles. The low Eames coffee table and the fibreglass armchair sit contentedly alongside a tri-legged wooden side table and a Mogens Koch cocktail trolley, unified by the open spaces created within and around their structural mass.

The living room's spacious alcove is used as a display area for furniture and decorative objects. A high wooden sideboard stows away the television and hi-fi behind sliding teak panels, while a well-preserved wall unit combines flexible shelving with modular cabinets. The lower drop-down cabinet door provides a small writing table when opened. The hardwood rocking chair recalls the classic style of Robsjohn-Gibbings, with a sloping seat and tilted backrest upholstered in wool. Opposite the rocker the polished surfaces of a trio of nesting tables crafted in rosewood reflect the diffused beam of the Poul Henningsen pendant lamp overhead. This quiet corner is a haven for mid-century classics, and, like the house itself, an unexpected refuge of enduring style.

Visiting clients are shown into the living room, but guests are ushered straight into the open-plan kitchen/dining area. The couple laid the floor with cork tiles and applied several coats of varnish to achieve a rich brown finish. In the dining area a Saarinen-inspired Arkana table is surrounded by four laminated-beech Jacobsen chairs designed in the 1950s and upholstered in

TOP FAR LEFT Textiles contribute hugely to a room's atmosphere. Here, a pair of square-end sofas upholstered in pseudo-suede cotton set around a wool rug provide a neutral backdrop for a range of colourful accessories.

BOTTOM FAR LEFT The generous sideboard and sleek cabinets in this wall unit combine storage space with attractive display surfaces. The shelves attest to the owners' passion for mid-century design: functional metalware, sculptural glassware and ceramic art sit alongside 1950s sourcebooks, period-style guides and encyclopedias of design.

LEFT An open-tread staircase, sleek woodwork and picture windows echo the streamlined shapes and minimalist pieces throughout this house. Although the owners fuse 1970s designs with 1950s classics, they have re-created a mid-century look that feels more contemporary than retro.

165

a fabric from Kvadrat in the 1970s. Perpendicular to the doorway, classic 1950s shelving is filled with mid-century glass and ceramics from Britain, Scandinavia, France, The Netherlands, Italy and Brazil. A spectacular display of abstract forms and functional Holmegaard and Riihimaki glassware is arranged on the shelves, the owner updating it with new finds as pieces are sold. In the kitchen area the stainless-steel and walnut cabinets were built in an understated contemporary style to suit the architecture. The surfaces are host to mid-century Dansk cookware from Jens Quistgaard, Bertel Gardberg's Canton stainless-steel and teak cooking pans, and ceramic tableware designed by Russel Wright and Eva Zeisel.In this house even the kitchen is a haven for mid-century classics, and, like the rest of the home, an unexpected refuge of enduring style.

[Classic mid-century pieces provide a visual link between the house's contrasting decorative styles.]

LEFT Upholstered dining chairs from Arne Jacobsen's Series 7 range are paired with a pedestal table.
ABOVE RIGHT No mid-century kitchen would be complete without Jens Quistgaard's teak-handled fondue pot and Kobenstyle saucepans for Dansk (1954).
RIGHT With a Jacob Bang Kastrup bottle vase, Hans Wegner chair and Josef Frank Loops fabric, the bedroom has a distinctly Scandinavian theme.

Collector's guide

Many prototypes of mid-century pieces and vintage originals were granted art status after being recognized as design classics, and have been collected by galleries and museums throughout the world. Limited editions and first-generation production runs are highly sought after, with works in ceramic and glass selling for premium prices. Glass by designers such as Ingeborg Lundin, Tapio Wirkkala and Sven Palmqvist rival the works of Muranese designers such as Fulvio Bianconi and Aldo Nason. Ceramics by the Natzlers, Stig Lindberg and Guido Gambone are in especially high demand.

Works in ceramic, glass and solid wood are usually worth more than those in veneer, wood inset with other materials, plaster or plastic. Factory-produced pottery and earthenware are generally of the same value as commercial china and can be identified by a hallmark on the base indicating the manufacturer and occasionally the designer or pattern. Complete sets of dinnerware are very rare, and sell for a high price, so many collectors build up a set over time, buying from dealers, markets or online auctions. Cutlery made from the type of stainless steel known as 18/10, which contains 18 per cent chrome and 10 per cent nickel, is usually found in excellent condition. Knives crafted in 13 per cent chrome with hardened blades are most likely to retain a sharp cutting edge. Satin and mirror-finished stainless steel pieces show small scratches and will have formed a patina similar to antique silver over time. Mid-century lamps may need rewiring but are often in good condition and are still relatively inexpensive. Lamps sold with their original shades are worth more. Expect to pay a premium of at least 25 per cent on a pair of lamps, chairs or glasses.

The value of vintages pieces by designers such as Eero Saarinen, Charles and Ray Eames, George Nelson, Gio Ponti, Arne Jacobsen and Hans Wegner is usually only 25–35 per cent higher than models that have been reintroduced and made today, making them a good investment. Originals produced in short runs are worth more than those produced in multiples, and works made in limited editions are especially prized. Many Danish designers made bespoke pieces for architects or private clients, and once provenance has been established, these sell for breathtaking figures.

The dating, signing and numbering of each piece determines its authenticity and value. While Scandinavian and American designers did this systematically, many designers were less methodical, resulting in huge price discrepancies between the designs that are authenticated and those that are only attributed to certain designers. Piero Fornasetti was notoriously indifferent to signing, dating or even numbering the items he produced, making the value of those that he authenticated frustratingly high.

Maintaining mid-century originals

Furniture and textiles require the least labour-intensive maintenance. Furniture should only be polished every seven to ten years, and then only sparingly. Avoid washing textiles, rugs, carpets and wall hangings, as they may discolour. Dry-clean vintage fabrics, but always tell the dry-cleaner the age of the fabric. The best way to freshen carpets and rugs is to lay them flat on newspaper or tissue paper and 'beat' them lightly with a special, bat-like carpet whisk. Do this on both sides, using fresh paper. Store carpets and textiles by rolling them flat around a cardboard tube or plastic cylinder, wrapping them in calico and placing them in a cool, dry cupboard. Vintage curtains should be brushed with a ponytail brush to remove as much dust as possible, then folded over a chair or table and vacuumed bit by bit in vertical downward strokes.

Vintage ceramics should hardly be washed at all. Glazed ceramics can be rinsed in water, but unglazed pieces should be spot-cleaned with a mild detergent. Avoid holding the item by the handle, its weakest point. Treat glassware as ceramics and avoid submerging them in water; use glassware cleaner for a clear, shiny surface.

Metalware benefits from frequent washing, but avoid dishwashing. Silver and stainless steel cutlery should be hand-washed in warm water with a mild soap or detergent, and then rinsed in clean, hot water and dried promptly. Dry cutlery thoroughly; never leave it to air-dry. Avoid using steel wool, bleach, scouring pads, silver-dip cleaners or any chemical not recommended for stainless steel. Note that most silver knives have stainless steel blades, as silver is too soft to craft into durable blades. Metal, wood and resinous cutlery should not be soaked for any length of time or left unwashed overnight. Chalky deposits on wood or resin handles can be removed by wiping them with cooking oil. Discoloration is usually easy to remove on high-quality metalware by rubbing it with a soapy cloth and drying immediately. If the stain persists, polish with a small amount of metal-cleaning cream. Store cutlery in a fitted canteen or in cloth cutlery rolls to prevent silver from tarnishing and other metals from rusting or rubbing against other pieces. Avoid mixing stainless steel with aluminium, silver-plate or sterling silver items in the same compartment or container.

Gilded products should be cleaned with soapy water rather than polish or cleaning solutions, as quality pieces were gilded with 24-carat gold compounds. Using polish eventually rubs off the platinum plating or gold. Take care not to let candles burn all the way down to the well and burn the metal. Pewter is beautiful and does not tarnish like silver, so all you need to use to keep it shiny is a soft sponge or cloth dipped in hot water. Dry the surface immediately and buff it with pewter polish.

Where to buy 1950s designs

A guide to recommended shops and dealers that specialize in vintage pieces, classic re-editions or contemporary designs created in the spirit of mid-century chic.

DEALERS, BOUTIQUES AND ONLINE DEALERS

ANGELA ADAMS DESIGN
273 Congress Street
Portland, ME 04101
USA
T +1 800 255 9454
www.angelaadams.com

ARAM
110 Drury Lane
London WC2B 5SG
England
T +44 (0)20 7557 7557
www.aram.co.uk

ARTEK
Eteläesplanadi 18
00010 Helsinki
Finland
T +44 (0)20 7420 5913
(UK sales office)
www.artek.fi

ATOMIC INTERIORS
Plumptre Square
Nottingham NG1 1JF
England
T +44 (0)115 941 5577
www.atomicinteriors.
co.uk

BABYLON
301 Fulham Road
London SW10 9QH
England
T +44 (0)20 7376 7255
www.babylonlondon.com

BOOMERANG FOR MODERN
2040 India Street
San Diego, CA 92101
USA
T +1 619 239 2040
www.boomerangformodern.
com

BOOM! INTERIORS
115–17 Regents Park Road
London NW1 8UR
England
T +44 (0)20 7722 6622
www.boominteriors.com

CENTURY
68 Marylebone High Street
London W1U 5JH
England
T +44 (0)20 7487 5100
www.centuryd.com

CHARTREUSE INTERNATIONAL
2609 First Avenue
Seattle, WA 98121
USA
T +1 206 328 4844

CHICKEN LITTLE
1323 Abbot Kenney Blvd
Los Angeles, CA 90291
USA
T +1 310 581 1676

CITY ISSUE
2825 Peachtree Road NE
Atlanta, GA 30305
USA
T +1 404 262 3500
www.cityissue.com

CLASSICON
Sigmund-Riefler-Bogen 3
81829 Munich
Germany
T +49 (0)89 74 81 33 0
www.classicon.com

COLE & SON
Lifford House
199 Eade Road
London N4 1DN
England
T +44 (0)20 8442 8844
www.cole-and-son.co.uk

COLLAGE 20TH CENTURY CLASSICS
1300 North Industrial Blvd
Dallas, TX 75207
USA
T +1 214 828 9888
www.collageclassics.com

DALTON'S AMERICAN
Decorative Arts
1931 James Street
Syracuse, NY 13206
USA
T +1 315 463 1568
www.daltons.com

DANICA
contact Gary Howard
T +44 07940 458890
www.danica.co.uk

DAVID MELLOR
4 Sloane Street
London SW1 8EE
England
T +44 (0)20 7730 4259
www.davidmellordesign.
com

DAVID RAGO AUCTIONS
333 North Main Street
Lambertville, NJ 08530
USA
T +1 609 397 9374
www.ragoarts.com

DECODENCE
1684 Market Street
San Francisco, CA 94102
USA
T +1 415 553 4521
www.decodence.com

DESIGN FOR DELIGHT
Jonkerplantsoen 2c
1508 EE Zaandam
T +31 (0)756 555 420
www.designfordelight.nl

DESIGNS OF DENMARK
88 Derby Road
Nottingham NG1 5FD
England
T +44 (0)115 948 4428
www.designsofdenmark.
com

EAMES OFFICE GALLERY & STORE
2665 Main Street
Santa Monica, CA 90405
USA
T +1 310 396 5991
www.eamesoffice.com

EAT MY HANDBAG BITCH GALLERY
37 Drury Lane
London WC2B 5RR
England
T +44 (0)20 7836 0830
www.eatmyhandbagbitch.
co.uk

ERA MID CENTURY FURNISHINGS & ART
7901 SE 13th Avenue
Portland, OR 97202
USA
T +1 503 234 1133
www.midcenturyera.
com

EUKLIDES 20TH CENTURY DESIGN
Pilestredet 75C
0354 Oslo
Norway
T +47 33 33 31 06
www.euklides.no

FANDANGO
50 Cross Street
London N1 2BA
England
T +44 (0)20 7226 1777
www.fandango.uk.com

FAT CHANCE
162 North La Brea Avenue
Los Angeles, CA 90036
USA
T +1 323 930 1960

FIGGJO
4332 Figgjo
Norway
T +47 5168 3534
www.figgjo.no

FORM VINTAGE MODERN
5330 College Avenue
Oakland, CA 94618
USA
T +1 510 420 1950

FRITZ HANSEN
Allerødvej 9
3450 Allerød
Denmark
T +45 4817 2300
www.fritzhansen.com

FUSION
30 Church Street
Birmingham B3 2NP
England
T +44 (0)121 236 1020
www.fusionlifestyle.co.uk

G P & J BAKER
North Dome
Chelsea Harbour
London SW10 0EX
England
T +44 (0)20 7351 7760
www.gpjbaker.com

GEORG JENSEN
15 New Bond Street
London W1S 3ST
England
T +44 (0)20 7499 6541
www.georgjensen.com

MONICA GLEREAN & VINCENZO CAFFARELLA
Alfie's Antique Market
(ground floor)
13–25 Church Street
London NW8 8DT
England
T +44 (0)20 7724 3701
www.vinca.co.uk

GOOD EYE 20TH CENTURY INTERIORS
4918 Wisconsin Avenue
Northwest
Washington, DC 20016
USA
T +1 202 244 8516
www.goodeyeonline.com

GUERIDON
359 Larayette Street
New York, NY 10012
USA
T +1 212 677 7740
www.gueridon.com

HENNESSEY & INGALLS
214 Wilshire Blvd
Santa Monica, CA 90401
USA
T +1 310 458 9074
www.hennesseyingalls.
com

HIGHBROW INC
2110 8th Avenue South
Nashville, TN 37204
USA
T +1 888 329 0219
www.highbrowfurniture.
com

HIVE
111 Northwest 2nd Avenue
Portland, OR 97209
USA
T +1 503 242 1967
www.hivemodern.com

HUDSON'S ANTIQUES
& FURNITURE GALLERY
1020 East 8th Street
Oakland, CA 94606
USA
T +1 510 645 5844
www.hudsonsgallery.
com

JETSET DESIGNS FOR
MODERN LIVING
at Broadway Antique
Market
6130 North Broadway
Chicago, IL 60660
USA
T +1 312 371 0986
www.jetsetmodern.com

JOBS HANDTRYCK
Västanvik 201
793 92 Leksand
Sweden
T +46 (0)247 122 22
www.jobshandtryck.se

LOS ANGELES
MODERN AUCTIONS
PO Box 462006
Los Angeles, CA 90046
USA
T +1 323 904 1950
www.lamodern.com

LOUIS POULSEN
Nyhavn 11
1001 Copenhagen
Denmark
T +45 3314 1414
www.louispoulsen.com

MAC LONDON
142 Clerkenwell Road
London EC1R 5DL
England
T +44 (0)20 7713 1234
www.mac-london.com

MAISONETTE
79 Chamberlayne Road
London NW10 3ND
England
T +44 (0)20 8964 8444
www.maisonette.uk.com

MARIMEKKO
Puusepänkatu 4
0800 Helsinki
Finland
T +358 9 75 871
www.marimekko.fi

MICHIGAN STREET
ANTIQUES CENTER
1049 East Michigan Street
Indianapolis, IN 46202
USA
T +1 317 972 8990

MIDCENTURY.MODERN
(fair for mid-century
classics and modern design)
contact Lucy Ryder
Richardson & Petra Curtis
tel +44 (0)20 8761 3405
www.ourshowhome.com

MIX GALLERY
17 South Main Street
Lambertville, NJ 08530
USA
T +1 609 733 0777
www.mix-gallery.com

MODERN WAY
2755 No. Palm Canyon
Palm Springs, CA 92262
USA
T +1 760 320 5455
www.psmodernway.com

MOD LIVIN'
5327 East Colfax Avenue
Denver, CO 80220
USA
T +1 720 941 9292
www.modlivin.com

MOMENTO DESIGN
Hjortevaenget 3
8270 Hoejbjerg
Denmark
T +45 7022 0074
www.momentodesign.dk

ONE DEKO LTD
Old Spitalfields Market
111-113 Commercial Street
London E1 6BG
England
T +44 (0)20 7375 3289
www.onedeko.co.uk

ORIGIN MODERNISM
25 Campden Passage
London N1 8EA
England
T +44 (0)20 7704 1326
www.origin101.co.uk

THE OTHER SHOP
327 Divisadero Street
San Francisco, CA 94117
USA
T +1 415 621 5424

OVERDOSE ON
DESIGN
182 Brick Lane
London E1 6SA
England
T +44 (0)20 7613 1266
www.overdoseondesign.
com

PLYWOOD TO PLASTIC
contact Nigel Wells
T +44 (0)7768 025 320
www.plywood2plastic.
co.uk

PRE VIEW
11 Southeast 6th Avenue
Delray Beach, FL 33483
USA
T +1 561 276 7640
www.previewmod.com

R 20TH CENTURY
DESIGN
82 Franklin Street
New York
NY 10013
USA
T +1 212 343 7979
www.r20thcentury.com

RICHARD SERRAULT
T +33 (0)69 9 46 33 03
www.epocepic.com

SCP
135-139 Curtain Road
London EC2A 3BX
England
T +44 (0)20 7739 1869
www.scp.co.uk

SHOWHOME
contact Lucy Ryder
Richardson and Petra
Curtis
T +44 (0)20 8761 3405
www.ourshowhome.
com

SKANK WORLD
7205 & 7221 Beverly Blvd
Los Angeles, CA 9036
USA
T +1 323 939 7858

SKYSCRAPER
237 East 60th Street
New York, NY 10022
USA
T +1 212 588 0644
www.skyscraperny.
com

SPRINGDALE
FURNISHINGS
19 South Elm Street
Three Oaks, MI 49128
USA
T +1 269 756 9896
www.sprindalefurnishings.
com

STELTON
Gammel Vartov Vej 1
2900 Hellerup
Denmark
T +45 3962 3055
www.stelton.dk

SUBLIME
402 North Palm Canyon
Drive
Palm Springs, CA 92262
USA
T +1 760 322 3286
www.sublimepalmsprings.
com

SVENSKT TENN
Strandvägen 5
114 84 Stockholm
Sweden
T +46 (0)8 670 1600
www.svenskttenn.se

THEMES AND
VARIATIONS
231 Westbourne Grove
London W11 2SE
England
T +44 (0)20 7727 5531
www.themeseandvariation.
com

20TH CENTURY
PROVENANCE
348 Broadway
Cambridge, MA 02139
USA
T +1 617 547 2300
www.20thcenturyprovenance.
com

TWENTYTWENTYONE
18c River Street
London EC1R 1XN
England
T +44 (0)20 7837 1900
www.twentytwentyone.
com

TWO COLUMBIA ROAD
2 Columbia Road
London E2 7NN
England
T +44 (0)20 7729 9933
www.twocolumbiaroad.
com

VESSEL
114 Kensington Park Road
London W11 2PW
England
T +44 (0)20 7727 8001
www.vesselgallery.com

VITRA
30 Clerkenwell Road
London EC1M 5PG
England
T +44 (0)20 7608 6200
www.vitra.com

ROBERT WELCH
Lower High Street
Chipping Campden
Gloucestershire GL55 6DY
England
T +44 (0)1386 840522
www.welch.co.uk

WIGERDALS VÄRLD
Krukmakargatan 14
118 51 Stockholm
Sweden
T +46 (0)8 31 64 04
www.wigerdal.com

Index

Author's acknowledgments

Many people share my enthusiasm for 1950s design, and many contributed to this project by sharing their ideas, contacts, knowledge and vision of why mid-century style is so contemporary today. I'd especially like to thank the team: Clare Limpus and Liz Boyd for tirelessly sourcing thousands of images, Alison Wormleighton for editing the manuscript with forensic lucidity, Megan Smith for coming up with yet another outstanding book design, Graham Atkins Hughes and Stellan Herner for taking fantastic photographs, and Zia Mattocks for being the hard-working superstar editor who held the whole project together. Friends everywhere came up with suggestions for great locations, but most of all I would like to thank Lucy Ryder Richardson, Petra Curtis, Gary Howard, Andrew Cussins, Jack and Esme Bonnington, Mats and Lisa Wigerdal, Alison Howell and Alex Kohner, Eri Aso, Birgitta Hosea, Lotta Lewenhaupt, Mette Baklund, Anna Maria Svensson, Amelia Coward, Max Fraser and Eva Branscome at the Twentieth Century Society. A special thanks to friends who lent 1950s designs from their shops to be photographed or let me borrow from their private collections: Bo Madestrand and Maria Friberg, Renée Kopal and Mark Meller, Nikolai Handeland at Euklides, Nadia Demetriou Ladas at Vessel, Bo and Morten at Momento, and Yvonne Sörensson at Svenskt Tenn.

Picture credits

The publisher would like to thank the following photographers, agencies and companies for their kind permission to reproduce the following photographs.

1 Minh & Wass; 5 Undine Prohl; 6–7 Matt Hranek/Art & Commerce Anthology Inc/courtesy of Wilsonart International; 10–11 Ray Main/Mainstream; 14 Julius Shulman (Garred Residence 1950, Architect: Caughey & Ternstrom); 15 Advertising Archives; 16 Julius Shulman (Sweeney Residence 1952, Architect: Rodney and Walker); 17 left Julius Shulman (Hayes Residence 1960, Architect: Raymond Kappe); 17 right Julius Shulman (Cooper Residence 1957, William Beckett); 18 Tim Street-Porter; 20–1 Roland Halbe (Architect: Alvar Aalto); 22 Mads Mogensen (Architect: Finn Juhl; Stylist: Martina Hunglinger); 23 Kim Ahm/House of Pictures (Architect: Arne Jacobsen); 25 RIBA Library Photographs Collection (Architect: Halldor Gunnlogsson); 26–7 Mark Luscombe-Whyte/The Interior Archive (Architect: Le Corbusier); 28 Advertising Archives; 29 RIBA Library Photographs Collection (Architect: Kenneth Wood); 30 Salvatore Licitra/Gio Ponti Archives (Architect: Gio Ponti); 32–3 Graham Atkins-Hughes; 36 David Glomb; 37 Tim Street-Porter/Elizabeth Whiting & Associates; 38 Peter Cook/View (Architect: Ludwig Mies van der Rohe); 39 David Glomb; 40 Andreas von Einsiedel (Architect: Chris Pearson); 41 Jean Luc Laloux; 42 Mark Luscombe-Whyte/Elizabeth Whiting & Associates; 43 Ray Main/Mainstream (Flying Duck Enterprises); 44 Ray Main/Mainstream; 45 above left Rasch Wallpapers; 45 above right, below left and right Conran Octopus (Wallpaper: Cole & Son); 46 Ray Main/Mainstream; 47 Tim Street-Porter; 48 left Trevor Mein (Architect: Dr Ernest Fooks); 48 right Ray Main/Mainstream; 49 Graham Atkins-Hughes; 50 above Gaelle le Boulicaut (Owner: Carina Enström-Gibbs; 50 below and 51 Graham Atkins-Hughes/Elle Decoration (styled by Atomic Interiors); 52 Peter Cook/View (Architect: Ludwig Mies Van Der Rohe); 53 Matt Hranek/Art & Commerce Anthology Inc/courtesy of Wilsonart International; 54 Bruce Hemming; 55 above Mads Mogensen (Stylist: Martina Hunglinger); 55 below Tim Street-Porter; 56 Trevor Mein; 57 Graham Atkins-Hughes; 58–9 Matt Hranek/Art & Commerce Anthology Inc/courtesy of Wilsonart International; 60 Tim Street-Porter/Elizabeth Whiting & Associates; 61 Ray Main/Mainstream; 62 twentytwentyone (Fabric design: Lucienne Day); 63 Ray Main/Mainstream; 64 left and right Conran Octopus (Wallpaper: G P & J Baker); 65 Ray Main/Mainstream; 67 above left and below left Conran Octopus; 67 above right and below right Marimekko Corporation; 68–9 Tim Street-Porter/Elizabeth Whiting & Associates; 70 Ray Main/Mainstream (Designer Craig Allen/Linley); 71 Paul Ryan/International Interiors; 72 left Vincent Leroux/Marie Claire Maison; 72 right Bruno Helbling/Zapaimages; 74 Tim Street-Porter/Elizabeth Whiting & Associates; 75 Geoff Lung; 76–7 Trevor Mein (Architect: Dr Ernest Fooks); 80 left Ray Main/Mainstream (Architect: Wells Mackereth); 80 right Ray Main/Mainstream; 81 and 82 above Tim Street-Porter; 82 below and 83 Ray Main/Mainstream; 84 James Merrell/Elle Decoration (styled by Tyger Design); 85–6 Ray Main/Mainstream; 87 Verne Fotografie; 88 above Reto Guntli/Zapaimages; 88 below Ken Hayden/Red Cover; 89 Tim Street-Porter/Elizabeth Whiting & Associates; 90 Tim Street-Porter; 91 Mikkel Vang; 92 Chris Tubbs/Red Cover; 94 above Tim Street-Porter; 94 below Geoff Lung; 95 Ray Main/Mainstream; 96 Tim Street-Porter; 97 Luc Wauman; 98 left Jake Curtis/Red Cover; 98 right Paul Ryan/International Interiors; 99 and 101 Minh & Wass; 102 Verne Fotografie; 103 Paul Ryan/International Interiors (Architect: Olle Rex); 104 Anson Smart; 105 left Henry Wilson/Red Cover; 105 right Graham Atkins-Hughes/Elle Decoration (styled by Atomic Interiors); 111 Minh & Wass (Shelf designer: Tyler Hays); 112 Ray Main/Mainstream; 113 Trevor Mein (Architect: Dr Ernest Fooks); 115 Louise Bobbe/Elle Decoration; 117 Ray Main/Mainstream; 118 below Ray Main/Mainstream (Designer: Shaun Clarkson); 119 Mark Williams/Elle Decoration; 120 James Merrell/Elle Decoration (styled by Tyger design); 121 left Ray Main/Mainstream; 126 above Graham Atkins-Hughes; 126 below Ray Main/Mainstream (Designer: Nick Monroe); 127 Graham Atkins-Hughes; 128 Undine Prohl; 131 Ray Main/Mainstream (Flying Duck Enterprises); 142–7 Michael Donnelly/Elizabeth Whiting & Associates (Architect: Richard Neutra); 158–9 and 160 above right Benny Chan (Architect: Richard Neutra, Restoration Architects: CJ Bonura); 160 above left, 160 below and 161 Art Gray (Architect: Richard Neutra, Restoration Architects: CJ Bonura)

The following photographs were specially commissioned by Conran Octopus:

Graham Atkins-Hughes: 73 (Owner: Gary Howard), 93 above (Owner: Gary Howard), 106–7 (Owner: Gary Howard), 110, 114, 116, 118 above, 121 right (Owner: Gary Howard), 122–5, 129 above (Architect: John S Bonnington), 129 below, 132–3, 136–41 (Architect: John S Bonnington) 152–7, 162–7 (Location: Showhome)

Stellan Herner: 2, 93 below, 130, 148–51 (Owners and Interior Designers: Lisa and Mats Wigerdal)

The publisher and author would like to thank the following mid-century specialists for their kind loan of furniture and accessories for photography. Contact details can be found on pages 170–1: Cole & Son, Danica, Euklides 20th Century Design, Figgjo, G P & J Baker, Jobs Handtryck, Momento Design, Showhome, Svenskt Tenn, Vessel and Wigerdals Värld.

Every effort has been made to trace the copyright holders. We apologize in advance for any unintentional omissions and would be pleased to insert the appropriate acknowledgment in any subsequent publication.